Published by

**NIYOGI
BOOKS**

D-78, Okhla Industrial Area, Phase-I
New Delhi-110 020, INDIA

Tel: 91-11-26816301, 26813350, 51, 52
Fax: 91-11-26810483, 26813830

email: niyogioffset@bol.net.in
www.niyogibooks.com

Author: Biswajit Roy Chowdhury

Designed by: Arvind
Cover Design: Navidita Thapa

ISBN: 978-81-89738-25-9

Year of Publication: 2008

Printed at: Niyogi Offset Pvt. Ltd, New Delhi, India

WILD
WONDERS
of india

Biswajit Roy Chowdhury

NIYOGI
BOOKS

To all who are keen
to protect our natural heritage.

CONTENTS

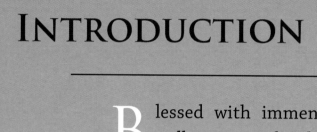

INTRODUCTION

B lessed with immense bio-diversity as well as geographical and cultural variety, India is truly unique. The majestic snow-clad Himalayan mountain range in the north, the vast expanse of the Thar Desert in the north-west, the Bay of Bengal in the south-east, the Arabian Sea in the south-west and the Indian Ocean in the south of the Indian Peninsula have all combined to make this country a treasure-trove of Nature's magnificent bounty.

Over the centuries, the diversity of Indian wildlife has influenced and also found representation in the culture, literature and art of the country.

In the earliest times man lived by hunting animals. It was his search for wild animals that led him from one place to another. With time, he domesticated some of these animals to serve his own requirements.

The first evidences of a township are found in the Indus Valley Civilisation (*Circa* 5000 BC). During excavations archaeologists unearthed, different animal figures like Tigers, Elephants and Bulls on seal carvings, terracotta and figurines in Mohenjodaro and Harappa, the two primary Indus Valley sites.

The people who lived in these Indus plains during 3000 BC-1800 BC were known as Aryans. It was during this period that Hindu philosophy was immortalised in a vast canon of literature, of which the four Vedas occupy a prime position.

Much of the Rig Veda is full of prayers to the natural deities like sun (*Surya*), fire (*Agni*), wind (*Vayu*), night (*Ratri*), among others. The Rig Veda demarcates life in four stages. These are: the *Brahmacharya* or the period where the *Shishya* or student had to go to the *Gurugriha* or *Gurukul* for tutelage. Here, in an *Ashram* (also the home of the Guru or teacher) located in idyllic surroundings, the student lived with his teacher till his education was complete. The second stage was *Grihastha* where the student entered family life and lived as a householder, fulfilling personal and social obligations. After this came *Vanaprastha*, when the same householder had to leave his children and material wealth and go to the forest for spiritual contemplation. It was during the fourth stage of *Sanyas* when he goes into solitude and meditation, in search of the truth behind his existence. Thus, the Vedic man spent a significant part of his life close to Nature.

Other than Hinduism, two great religions or philosophies originated in India around 6th century BC. Buddhism, founded by Prince Siddharth, later known as Gautam Buddha and Jainism founded by Mahavir. Both these religions promulgated teachings of non-violence and co-existence with wildlife and Nature.

During the reign of the great Emperor Ashoka in the 8th century BC, the first norms of wildlife preservation came into force. Ashoka imposed a ban on hunting certain animals and birds during specific seasons. He also spread his message of non-violence and peaceful co-existence with animals. The emblem of Emperor Ashoka, which has the figure of the Lion on four sides, has become the National Emblem of India. It is known as the 'Ashoka Stambh'.

The perspective towards wildlife changed immensely with the Mughal invasion of India in the 16th century AD. Hunting of wild animals on horseback or elephant-back became a sporting event and that marked the beginning of the destruction of India's wildlife. Humayun and Jahangir were the two emperors who were especially fond of hunting wild animals, mainly Tigers, during their regimes.

During the early 19th century, the wealthy Muslim rulers of small states, known as the Nawabs and their Hindu counterparts, the

Maharajas, indulged in the sport of hunting wild animals. Most of them had their own hunting grounds where outsiders, except for the royal guests, were not allowed to enter or hunt.

The year 1857 marked the beginning of the Victorian era in Indian history. Viceroys and high officials appointed by the royal rulers in India considered hunting a mark of bravery. During this period itself, within a span of 25 years, John Yule slew 400 Tigers, the Maharaja of Rewa 500 Tigers, Maharaja Shamsur Jung 433 Tigers and the Prime Minister of Nepal, killed 300 Tigers.

But even in pre-independent India there were dedicated wildlife lovers like Jim Corbett. An Englishman born in India, Jim Corbett is famous for having hunted man-eating Tigers and Leopards in today's Uttarakhand. Eventually Jim Corbett gave up hunting under the influence and advice of a British forest officer FW Champion and became a pioneer of India's wildlife conservation.

Champion pioneered the skill of shooting wild animals with a camera instead of the gun. Later many maharajas, nawabs and estate-owners started an initiative to conserve wildlife in their own game reserves. In this respect, the Maharaja of Rewa in Madhya Pradesh, Maharaja Bhanjdeo of Orissa, Billy Arjan Singh of Uttar Pradesh, the Nawab of Junagarh, the Maharaja of Ramgarh in Chattisgarh and the Maharaja of Jaipur in Rajasthan are worth mentioning.

After India attained Independence in 1947, small states were merged with the sovereign Indian Union. The rapid development of India in terms of industrialisation, urbanisation, communication network and building of heavy dams and factories was at the cost of wildlife. Also, hunting became rampant and commoners also indulged in it ruthlessly.

According to information gathered from various literature and books written by hunters and naturalists, it is estimated that by the turn of the 20th century at least 40,000 to 50,000 tigers used to roam the jungles of India, in spite of merciless hunting by the Mughals, the maharajas, the nawabs, the British rulers and ordinary hunters. Unfortunately, despite the launch of intensive protection programmes through different statutes framed by the Government of India and implementation of the 'Project Tiger', the number of this majestic animal has gone down to around 1,400 at present.

Though some wildlife and forest laws framed by the British existed even before Independence, the real ban on hunting was imposed after the Wildlife (Protection) Act, 1972, came into force.

With its diverse landscape, various ecosystems and wildlife, India is not only geographically unique but also an ideal haven of diverse fauna and flora. There are about 500 species of mammals, 1,300 varieties of birds, 530 kinds of reptiles, 140 species of amphibians, more than 200 species of fishes, about 4,000 varieties of mollusks and over 50,000 forms of insects.

Wild Wonders of India provides an account of India's varied wildlife—its birds and animals, some already extinct, some on the threshold of extinction—urging us to live and let live.

Tiger Reserves & National Parks of India

Biogeographic Zones

Trans Himalayas	Gangetic Plains	Desert	Western Ghats	Islands
Himalayas	Semi Arid	Deccan Peninsula	Coasts	North East

Map not to scale. Boundaries of India, states and locations indicative only.

ANIMALS AND THEIR FAMILIES

As we humans group together and live in families, animals too have their families defined. Just as human beings related by blood show certain common physical and biological characteristics, animals belonging to the same family show common physical, breeding or biological patterns.

The Royal Bengal or Indian Tiger *(Panthera tigris tigris)*, one of the foremost members of the cat family, is an animal, which has aroused the concern of conservationists throughout the globe. In order to save this graceful animal, Project Tiger was initiated in 1973 in nine Protected Areas. At present, there are 27 Tiger Reserves spread over 40,000 sq km of Tiger habitats in India.

The Tiger has a brilliant yellowish-orange coat patterned with black stripes. These patterns differ between individuals. Two Tigers can also be differentiated by the variation in their facial markings. The Tiger's tail is long and banded. It has two white patches on the back of its ear-tips. Its body weight ranges between 140 to 250 kg and length (from the tip of the nose to the tail tip) is 2.7 to 3.3 m.

Tigers generally delineate their own territory. The male demarcates its territory by spraying a scent, known as pheromone, on tree trunks and rocks. It also marks its territory by scratching the tree trunks with its nails. Females too mark their territory by spraying. When the Tigress is physically ready to mate, the scent attracts males.

The courtship period continues for a maximum of two weeks. The gestation period is about 100 to 110 days. The litter size varies between one and six. The Tiger is usually a solitary animal except during mating time. Young adults are sometime found roaming along with the mother; otherwise socialising amongst Tigers is a rare yet joyful sight.

While giving birth, the Tigress separates itself from the male in some lonely place. Rearing and upbringing of cubs are the responsibilities of the mother alone.

Usually cubs remain with the mother for 16 to 20 months, after which they choose their own territories and get separated from their mother.

The Tiger is a carnivore and feeds on Deer, Antelopes, Wild Pigs and even birds like Peafowl. There are many records of Tigers devouring Leopards. In the Sunderbans, due to hostile topography, Tigers are even known to eat fishes and Crabs. Very rarely do Tigers turn man-eaters. The reasons why a Tiger is sometimes forced to turn into a man-eater are mentioned ahead.

Left: The majestic White Tiger.
Pages 14-15: The Royal Bengal Tiger or Indian Tiger.

The Snow Leopard is found in the high-altitude snow-clad regions of the Himalayas.

- When it becomes old and incapable of hunting its normal prey.
- If, for any reason, it loses its canines or injures its paw.
- If it is of a litter of a man-eater, it develops the habit of eating human flesh since birth.

Many people are of the opinion that most of the Tigers in the Sunderbans are man-eaters. But this notion is completely wrong. Due to hostile conditions of the area, humans have become one of the items in its food chain. Apart from that the Tiger is rarely a habitual man-eater.

A highly adaptable animal, the Tiger is found in all sorts of climatic conditions like evergreen, deciduous, dry scrub forests as well as in colder regions and swampy mangrove forests.

In order to save the dwindling Tiger population, Project Tiger was launched in 1973 in nine National Parks and Wildlife Sanctuaries. Now there are 27 Tiger Reserves spread all over the country. The total numbers of wild Tigers left in India today is only around 1,400. The Tiger is highly threatened because of poaching and an ever-increasing demand for its 'vital' body-parts.

The White Tiger is neither a different species nor is it an albino; it is the genetic manifestation of a 'recessive allele', that is, a hidden genetic character which appears because of a combination of certain genetic sequences.

The Leopard (*Panthera pardus*) is an elegant cat with a yellow coat and black rosettes on it. The length varies between 1.90 and 2.15 m and its body weight is between 40 and 68 kg. It is one of the most agile hunters and an expert in climbing trees and is mostly nocturnal in its activities. It feeds on Deer, Antelopes, rodents, domestic Hens, Ducks, cattle, lesser carnivores and herbivores. Pariah Dogs are one of its favourite foods. In India, this beautiful cat is found all over the country. Usually it stalks in the fringes of the forest villages to procure its prey. Fossils indicate that Leopards migrated to India much before Tigers. Since they are found in Sri Lanka as well, it indicates that they arrived before Sri Lanka was separated from the Indian mainland.

The colour-mutated Black Panthers are also seen in Indian forests. The Black Panthers (a melanistic form), less commonly known as Black Leopards, have the same distribution as that of Leopards.

The Snow Leopard *(Uncia uncia)* is a cat found in high altitudes. This furry creature has a pale yellowish-grey coat with dark grey rosettes. Its length is between 1 to 1.3 m and it weighs between 35 to 55 kg. It feeds on high-altitude herbivores like Bharals and Ibexes and even birds. The Snow Leopard is so named because it is found in the snow-clad mountain regions and rarely descends below 2,130 m. It is seen in the Himalayan alpine forests from Kashmir in the west to Arunachal Pradesh in the north-east.

The Leopard Cat *(Prionailurus bengalensis)* is found widely distributed throughout the forests of India. It is about the size of a domestic cat. It resembles a miniature form of the Leopard. But instead of rosettes, it has black spots all over the body. It feeds on birds and lesser mammals of the forests and usually hunts in the vicinity of villages. The Leopard Cat is less shy than other wild cats.

The Fishing Cat *(Prionailurus viverrina)* is much bigger than the Leopard Cat and more aggressive

The Black Panther is a colour-mutated form of the common Leopard (Panthera pardus).

in nature. The colour of its body is tawny-grey with stripes on its head and nape. There are bands on its tail. The Fishing Cat feeds on fishes, reptiles, domestic Goats, Sheep and other smaller mammals. Its preferred habitats are swampy and marshy areas.

The Jungle Cat *(Felis chaus)* is the most common wild cat of the Indian forests. The colour of its coat is tawny-yellow and the tail is short. It has tufts of hair on the tip of its ears. It hunts domestic and poultry birds and even calves of goats, lesser mammals, and birds.

Bottom left: The Leopard Cat, about the size of a domestic cat, is found in almost all parts of India.

Bottom right: A Fishing Cat cub.

The Rusty-spotted Cat *(Prionailurus rubiginosa)* is smaller in size than the Leopard Cat which is closely related to it. It has fawn-grey spots on its body. Though it is known to be found from Madhya Pradesh to peninsular India, there are records of its sighting in Kashmir as well. This species of cat has become a rarity.

In the Civet family the Common Palm Civet *(Paradoxurus hermaphroditus)* and the Small Indian Civet *(Viverricula indica)* yield perfume-like scent.

Asiatic Elephants *(Elephas maximus)* belong to the mammalian order *'Proboscidea'*. They are distributed in four separate geographical zones, such as south India (Tamil Nadu, Karnataka, Kerala and Andhra Pradesh), north India (Uttar Pradesh and Uttarakhand), east India (Orissa,

Elephants are threatened due to shrinking habitats and poaching for tusks.

southern West Bengal and Bihar) and north-east India (Northern West Bengal, Assam, Arunachal Pradesh, Meghalaya, Nagaland, Manipur and Tripura). There are evidences to show that during the Indus Valley Civilisation in the 3rd and 2nd millennium BC, Elephants were found all over India except the mangrove forests and higher ridges of the Himalayas.

Elephants are migratory by nature and they move in herds from one forest to another in search of fodder. Due to rampant deforestation the corridors through which elephants migrate, have been destroyed. As a result of this, Elephants are forced to enter human habitations, which invariably leads to man-animal conflict. Elephants are intelligent creatures and have sharp memories. A trained Elephant in captivity can respond to about 40 commands at a time. They are highly sociable and follow a matriarchal form of society. The oldest and largest female usually becomes the leader of the herd. Generally, a typical family herd will have 10 or more Elephants. Sometimes due to in-fighting among two bulls, one gets ousted from the herd and becomes a loner. Elephants in 'musth' display aggressive behaviour and therefore can prove to be dangerous during that period.

The gestation period of an elephant is 18 to 22 months. Elephants usually become sexually mature by 14 to 15 years of age. Females are capable of conceiving till the age of 60 years. When the calf is born, the entire family guards it till it can defend itself from predators like Tigers and Panthers. The life expectancy of an Elephant is usually 70 to 80 years.

The largest member of the Bovine family of India is the Gaur *(Bos gaurus)*. It is a robust Wild Ox with the adult male sporting a big hump on the shoulder. The Gaur's body is black and legs are white below the knees. It prefers forested areas away from human habitation. The animal is found throughout the country though loss of habitat is a major threat to its survival. Another big Wild Ox is the Yak *(Bos grunniens)*. A heavy coat of fur enables it to inhabit the cold regions of the western and north-eastern Himalayas.

The Asiatic Wild Buffalo *(Bubalus bubalis)* is a magnificently built animal with huge horns. It is probably the most powerful animal among the members of the Bovine family. This animal is found in the forests of north-east India, and in the Bastar district of Madhya Pradesh.

Apart from endemic primates, animals like the Rhesus Macaque *(Macaca mulatta)* are found all

The Gaur is the biggest member of the Indian Bovine family.

over the country. It moves in large troops under the leadership of a dominant male. It often enters human habitations and damages orchards and farms, which ends up creating a man-animal conflict. Among Langurs, Hanuman Langurs *(Presbytis entellus)* are the commonest. The colour of its coat is yellowish-cream to white and it has a long tail. Its face, palms and feet are black. Hanuman Langurs are commonly found around temples and create panic among pilgrims by snatching their food.

Forests of India harbour nine species of the Cervidae family. Characteristically, Deer shed their antlers every year unlike the Antelopes. The most common amongst the Indian Deer are the beautiful Chitals *(Axis axis)*. They are distributed throughout the country. Both the

Wild Buffaloes are magnificently built animals with huge sweeping horns.

sexes of this spectacular ungulate have white spots on brown to dark-brown bodies. Males sport antlers while the females do not develop antlers. Grasslands are the favoured habitats of Chitals and they feed on grass, leaves and fruits. In the meadows of Kanha, Chitals are found in massive groups. The forests of Western Ghats, Eastern Ghats, Maharashtra, Gangetic Plains and mangrove swamps are some of the Chital's ideal habitats.

The Sambar (*Cervus unicolor*) is another common animal belonging to the deer species. Males develop long antlers, which grow up to 125 cm or even 150 cm in length. Its body coat varies from earth-brown to tawny-brown. The Sambar's food habits is much like any other deer species. It is commonly found in the forests of Western and Eastern Ghats, Gangetic Plains, north-eastern forests and peninsular India. Chitals and Sambars constitute the bulk of food for the big carnivores of these forests.

The Muntjac (*Muntiacus muntjac*) or the Barking Deer, is much smaller in size than the Chital. Its coat is chestnut-brown and male's antlers are small, each having two branches. It is a shy animal and is found in all types of forests, except for the Sunderbans mangroves.

Closely related to the Chital is the Hog Deer (*Axis pocinus*). The stag possesses a three-point antler like the Chital. The favourite habitats of the Hog Deer are the riverine grasslands of Kaziranga, Corbett, Dudhwa, Jaldapara, Manas and Orang.

The Chital is the most common Deer of the country.

The Hard-ground Barasinga is found only in Kanha Tiger Reserve in Madhya Pradesh.

The Barasinga (*Cervus duvauceli*) has three sub-species in India. One is known as the Hard-ground Barasinga (*Cervus duvauceli branderi*), found in Kanha Tiger Reserve and the other two are called Soft-ground Barasinga (*Cervus duvauceli ranjitsinhi* and *Cervus duvauceli duvauceli*), which are residents of Kaziranga National Park and Manas Tiger Reserve in Assam, and Dudhwa Tiger Reserve and Pilibhit forests in Uttar Pradesh. Once the number of the Hard-ground Barasinga came down to 66 in Kanha. But due to intensive conservation efforts, it has now gone up to over 500. The colour of its coat varies from yellowish-brown to earth-brown depending on the season. The stag stands 127 cm high. The Barasinga is so named because an adult male's antlers can have 12 or more pointed branches ('*bara*' means twelve and '*sing*' means horns in Hindi).

The Indian Chevrotain or Mouse Deer (*Moschiola meminna*) is the smallest member of the Deer family. It has large hooves, long canines and an arched posture when standing. Neither the male nor the female has antlers. The body coat is speckled olive-brown. It can be best seen in Mudumalai Wildlife Sanctuary in Tamil Nadu and Bandipur National Park in Karnataka.

The Nilgai or the Blue Bull is the biggest Antelope of India.

The Musk Deer (*Moschus chrysogaster*) has no facial gland but it sports a musk gland. Its canines are long and exposed. The ears are long and the colour of the body coat is brownish-yellow with white lower legs. Found in Assam, Arunachal Pradesh and Garhwal Himalayas, it is heavily poached for its musk.

Six species of Antelopes are found in India. They do not have canines but possess permanent horns that never shed.

The Nilgai or Blue Bull (*Boselaphus tragocamelus*) is the largest among the antelope family of India. The male has a greyish-blue coat. It resembles a horse with two small horns. The female is tawny-brown in colour. They have white rings on the ankles. It is a herbivorous animal seen in northern, western and central India. In some areas it causes immense damage to crops which invariably leads to a man-animal conflict.

The Blackbuck (*Antilope cervicapra*) is a close kin of the African Impala. It is found only in the Indian subcontinent. The body of the male is black from head to back and the underparts are white. It has two long spiral shaped horns. The upper parts of the female are tawny-brown. It is distributed throughout the plains of India.

The Four-horned Antelope (*Tetracerus quadricornis*), commonly known as Chausinga, is a small-sized light-brown Antelope. The adult male sports two pairs of antlers. It is distributed throughout the dry forest of the country, mainly south of the gangetic plains. Loss of habitat and poaching are the main threats to its survival.

The Chinkara *(Gazella bennettii)* is almost of the same size as the Four-horned Antelope. It is the only antelope of India where both sexes have horns. The male has curved and ringed horns while the female has smaller irregular shaped horns. The upper part of the body is light brown and the underparts are white. It is found in parts of north, central and western India.

The Tibetan Gazelle *(Procapra picticaudata)* is a small antelope with antlers curved backwards. It is found in Ladakh and Sikkim. The Tibetan Gazelle is a highly endangered species.

The Chiru or Tibetan Antelope *(Pantholops hodgsonii)*, has a luxuriant coat that keeps it warm in very cold temperatures. This coat is used to produce the 'Shahtoosh' wool (legally banned by the governments of India, Pakistan and China). A

Right: The Blackbuck is found only in the Indian subcontinent.

Bottom: The Goral is a wild mountain goat.

highly-priced woollen shawl is made out of the Shahtoosh wool.

Production and possession of these shawls is prohibited by law as it is for these that Chirus are poached mercilessly in their habitats. In India they can be seen in the Chang Chen Mo Valley of Ladakh.

Among the Canaidae family of India, the Wild Dog or Dhole *(Cuon alpinus)* is a forest dog with a

reddish-brown coat and a black bushy tail. It is an agile hunter and hunts in a pack. It prefers dry open-wooded country and grasslands. Some of the best places to see Wild Dogs are Kanha National Park, Bandhavgarh National Park, Tadoba National Park, Nagarhole National Park and Bandipur National Park.

The Grey Wolf *(Canis lupus)* resembles a slim German Shepard dog. Its grey coat is interspersed with black and its underparts are buff. As its food

The Grey Wolf resembles a slim German Shepard Dog.

Facing page: The Golden Jackal can be often spotted near human habitation.

includes domestic livestock, it often leads to man-animal conflict. It is distributed throughout India except for the north-eastern states and lower peninsula. The Tibetan Wolf *(Canis lupus chanco)* is larger than the Indian Wolf with a whitish furry coat. It is found in Himachal Pradesh and Kashmir. The Golden Jackal *(Canis aureus)* is a rough-coated

buff-grey animal with a greyish, bushy tail. From a distance, it may sometimes be confused with a Wolf. It is an efficient hunter and sometimes takes to scavenging. Distributed throughout the country, the Golden Jackal inhabits urban and semi-urban areas. Destruction of habitat poses a major threat to its survival.

The Red Fox *(Vulpes vulpes)* is covered with reddish fur. The tail is long and bushy with a white tip. It is smaller than a Wild Dog or Jackal. Three sub-species of foxes are found in India—the Kashmir Fox *(V.v. griffithi)*, the

Tibetan Fox *(V.v. montana)* and the Desert Fox *(V.v. pusilla)*. Foxes feed on domestic hens, goats and lesser mammals.

The Indian or Bengal Fox is smaller than the Red Fox. Its ears are longer than that of its red counterpart and the tail has a black tip. Foxes have become an endangered species due to loss of their habitat and growing urbanisation.

Facing page: The Slow Loris is found in the evergreen forests of north-eastern India.

The Wild Pig is found in almost all forests of India.

The Striped Hyena *(Hyaena hyaena)* has a sloping back, a buff body with black stripes and a bushy tail. The Hyena is usually a scavenger and a carnivore. It is found in almost all parts of India. It is frequently seen in the Gir National Park. Road accidents and poaching are the main threats to the Hyenas survival.

Among the Ursidae family, the commonest member is the Sloth Bear *(Melursus ursinus)*. It is a black Bear with long fur. The Sloth Bear has a white 'V' shaped mark on the throat. It feeds on Termites, Ants and often scavenges on kill made by other carnivores. The Sloth Bear is distributed throughout the country except the high

The Indian Tree Shrew scanning the forest intently.

Himalayas, Jammu and Kashmir and arid areas of Rajasthan and Gujarat.

The Himalayan Brown Bear *(Ursus arctos)* is the largest member of India's bear family. It is a large bear with a thick, reddish-brown coat and no clear chest markings that are present in most other bears. It prefers the alpine scrubs and meadows of Himachal Pradesh and Kashmir. Poaching is the prime threat to its existence.

The Himalayan or Asiatic Black Bear *(Ursus thibetanus)* is larger than the Sloth Bear and prefers the forested habitats of the Himalayas. It has a white and very prominent 'V' on the upper chest. It is basically arboreal but does not sleep on trees. It is distributed in the forests of the north-east, east India and Jammu and Kashmir.

India has three members of the family Suidae: the Wild Pig *(Sus scrofa)*, the Andaman Hog and the Pygmy Hog *(Sus salvanius)*. The Pygmy Hog is a seriously endangered animal and falls in the Critically Endangered category of the Red Data Book of International Union for Conservation of Nature and Natural Resources (IUCN). It is restricted to the Manas Tiger Reserve. The Wild Pig, on the other hand, are found throughout India.

The Slender Loris *(Loris lyddekerianus)* occurs in the forests of southern India and the bigger member of the Loridae family, the Slow Loris *(Nycticebus bengalensis)*, is found in the dense forests of north-eastern India.

There are three Tree Shrews found in India. They are the South Indian or Madras Tree Shrew *(Anathana ellioti)*, the Common Tree Shrew *(Tupaia glis)* and the Nicobar Tree Shrew *(Tupaia nicobarica)*.

The Common Indian Grey Mongoose *(Herpestes edwardsii)* and the Small Indian Mongoose *(Herpestes javanicus)* are fairly common and usually found all over the country. The Ruddy Mongoose *(Herpestes smithii)* is found in north and peninsular India, the Crab-eating Mongoose *(Herpestes urva)* is usually an inhabitant of north-eastern states and the Marsh Mongoose *(Herpestes palustris)* is endemic to the wetlands of eastern Kolkata.

Top: The Small-clawed Otter is the smallest of all Indian Otters.

Above left: The Rufous-tailed Hare is common to almost all Indian forests.

Otters, which belong to the Mustelidae family, have three species in the country among which the most common is the Smooth Coated Otter (*Lutrogale perspicillata*). The Common or Eurasian Otter (*Lutra lutra*) is found in Kashmir, the Himalayan ranges and peninsular India. The Small-clawed Otter (*Amblonyx cinereus*) is so named because of its rudimentary claws. It is found in the western, eastern and north-eastern Himalayas and Coorg and Nilgiri ranges in the south.

Three species of Martens are found in India, among which the Beech Marten (*Martes foina*) and the Yellow-throated Marten (*Martes flavigula*) are Himalayan species and the Nilgiri Marten (*Martes gwatkinsi*) is found in the Nilgiris.

The Ferret Badgers are considered a mixture of a ferret and a badger and are found in the north-eastern states. The Hog Badger (*Arctonyx collaris*) also occurs in north-eastern India. The Black and White Honey Badger or the Indian Ratel (*Mellivora capensis*) is found all over the country.

The ant-eater family consists of two members. The Indian Pangolin (*Manis crassicaudata*) occurs all over India and the Chinese Pangolin (*Manis pentadactyla*), is found in the north-eastern states and northern West Bengal.

Many species of Wild Hares are found throughout the country, among which the most rare and endangered is the Hispid Hare (*Caprolagus hispidus*). It is seen in the forests of Terai and the Duars. The commonest Hare is the Indian or Black-naped Hare (*Lepus nigricollis*), which has a sub-species, namely the Rufous-

The Royle's Pika looks like a tail-less big rat and is found in the upper regions of the Himalayas.

Right: The Five-striped Palm Squirrel is the commonest of all Indian squirrels.

tailed Hare *(Lepus nigricollis ruficaudatus)*. The Desert Hare *(Lepus nigricolis dayanus)* inhabits the dry zones of Rajasthan, Punjab and Gujarat.

The Himalayan Marmot *(Marmota himalayana)* and the Long-tailed Marmot *(Marmota caudata)* are residents of the Garhwal Himalayas, Ladakh, Kashmir and Sikkim and are found at an altitude of 4,300 m.

While the Five-striped Palm Squirrel *(Funambulus pennantii)* is the most common, the Three-striped Palm Squirrel *(Funambulus palmarum)* is a well-distributed species, though it is rarer than the Five-striped ones. The Himalayan Squirrel family includes the Orange-bellied Himalayan Squirrel *(Dremomys lokriah)*, the Hoary-bellied Himalayan Squirrel *(Callosciurus pygerythrus)* and the Malayan Giant Squirrel *(Ratufa bicolor)*. Peninsular India harbours two endemic varieties of squirrels: the Malabar Giant Squirrel *(Ratufa indica)* and the Grizzled Giant Squirrel *(Ratufa macroura)*.

Many varieties of flying squirrels are found all over India. The Woolly Flying Squirrel is among

Top left: Himalayan Marmots are common in Ladakh.

Top right: The Grizzled Giant Squirrel is one of the most uncommon member of the squirrel family.

Pages 36-37: Rat Snakes help in preserving food grain by devouring field rats.

the largest and is almost 105 cm long. In Kashmir and Sikkim, the Woolly Flying Squirrel *(Eupetaurus cinereus)* is seen. Other than these there are the Red Giant Flying Squirrel *(Petaurista petaurista)*, the Indian Giant Flying Squirrel *(Petaurista phillipensis)*, the Hairy-footed Flying Squirrel *(Belomys pearsoni)* and the Travancore Flying Squirrel *(Petinomys fuscocapillus)*.

Another very important member of the Indian Rodentia family is the Porcupine. The hair of the porcupine have evolved in the form of long spikes, which act as its defence. The Indian Porcupine *(Hystrix indica)* is distributed throughout the country. The Himalayan Crestless or the Hodgson's Porcupine *(Hystrix brachyura)* is seen in West Bengal and Assam at an altitude of 1,525 m or above.

The Long-eared or Collared Hedgehog *(Hemiechinus collaris)* and the Indian or Pale Hedgehog *(Paraechinus micropus)* are found in the dry regions of Rajasthan and Gujarat.

Both fruit-eating and carnivorous bats are found throughout the country. Among many species of bats, the commonest are the Indian Flying Fox *(Pteropus giganteus)* and the Indian Pipistrelle *(Pipistrellus coromandra)*. The Fulvous Fruit Bat *(Rousettus leschenaulti)*, the Greater False Vampire Bat *(Megaderma lyra)* and the Great Indian or Woolly Horse-shoe Bat *(Rhinolophus luctus)* are some of the other species of bats.

The formidable King Cobra, now endangered.

The world of reptiles includes many species of Snakes, Crocodiles, Turtles and Lizards. The most venomous Snake is the King Cobra *(Ophiophagus hannah)* which has become endangered. Among other venomous Snakes are the Indian Cobra *(Naja naja)*, which comprises two sub-species—the Spectacled Cobra and the Monocellate Cobra. The Common Indian Krait *(Bungarus caeruleus)*, the Banded Krait *(Bungarus fasciatus)*, the Russell's Viper *(Vipera russelli)*, the Saw-scaled Viper *(Echis carinata)*, the Green or Bamboo Pit Viper *(Trimeresurus gramineus)* and many other species of marine Snakes are found in the country. Among non-venomous Snakes are the Rat Snake, the Vine Snake, the Bronze-tree Snake, the Ornamental Snake, the Wolf Snake, the Common Kukri Snake, the Sand Boa, the Red Boa and many others.

Out of the three types of Crocodiles the Estuarine Crocodile *(Crocodylus porosus)* is one, the length of which sometimes exceeds 17 ft. The ideal places to observe these Crocodiles are the Sunderbans in West Bengal and Bhitarkanika in Orissa. Another big species is the Marsh Crocodile *(Crocodylus palustris)*, which is found all

over the country. The most unique species is the Gharial *(Gavialis gengeticus)*. This fish-eating species has a long snout. Gharials occur in the Ganga, the Chambal, the Brahmaputra and their tributaries.

Twenty-six species of freshwater Turtles are found in India. These include *Lissemys punctata, Melanochelys tricarinata, Geoclemys hamiltoni, Kachuga sylhentensis K. tecta, K. smithi, Geochelone travancorica, Kachuga* and others. The most prominent of all Sea Turtles, which come to the coasts of India, is the Olive Ridley Turtle *(Lepidochelys olivacia)*. It visits the coasts of the

Gharials are endemic to the Indian subcontinent.

Bay of Bengal, specially the beaches of Rashikulya in Orissa. Other Sea Turtles include the Leather-backed Turtle *(Dermochelys coriacea)* and the Hawksbill Turtle. The Lizard family has over 100 members in the country. Geckos *(Hemidactylus)* are very common. Garden Lizards *(Calotes versicolor)* and Chamelions *(Chameleo zeylanicus)* are found throughout India. The 6-ft-long Water Monitor Lizard *(Varanus salvator)* is very common in the Sunderbans and swamps of Orissa.

The lesser species, the Bengal Monitor Lizard, is found throughout. The smallest Monitor Lizard, the Yellow Varanas *(Varanus flavescens),* is found in eastern and northern India.

Among the many amphibian species, the Himalayan Salamander or Newt, is the only amphibian species with a tail. It occurs in Namthing Pokhri, Sonada, Mirik and Margaret's Hope Tea Garden in Darjeeling district and in some pockets of Sikkim.

Different species of Toads and Frogs also occur in the country, among which the most beautiful and unique are the Leaping Tree Frogs.

To sum up, there is no doubt that India's wildlife wealth is unparalleled. However, the truth that stares us in the face today is that many of our wildlife species are greatly endangered, thanks to illegal hunting and poaching.

We need to act now, otherwise, a day may soon be near, when mankind is left with nothing but barren spaces.

The Indian Rock Python is a non-venomous snake that constricts its prey.

BIRDS AND THEIR HABITAT

Species variation of birds depends on their habitats. For example, Great Hornbills are found in dense forests where there are tall trees. Curlews are found on shores, Moorhens in swamps, Monals in the Upper Himalayas, Bengal Floricans in grasslands and Great Indian Bustards in arid regions.

Forests are the most important bird habitats. According to *BirdLife International,* more than 50 percent of the globally threatened bird species of the subcontinent are forest dwellers. Not only that, two-thirds of the endemic bird species of the subcontinent depend on forests for their survival.

The Indian subcontinent is home to many miles of forests and jungles. At the top, it starts with the alpine and sub-alpine forests of Juniper and Fir of the Himalayas and then coming gradually downwards, there are the dry coniferous forests of Pine, Moist Oak, Rhododendron and further down in the Himalayan foothills are the moist and dry deciduous forests.

In the plains, on one hand the forest extends upto the mangroves of India and on the other hand, covering central India and Maharashtra, forested areas reach the Western Ghats in peninsular India and Andaman and Nicobar Islands. Rich tropical evergreen forests are found in the north-eastern Himalayas, Western Ghats, and the Andaman and Nicobar Islands. Grasslands are another important habitat of birds. Vast grasslands are seen in the foothills of the Himalayas which are known as Terai in Assam and Uttarakhand, and Duars in West Bengal. Many of these grasslands get flooded during rains by the water of the mighty rivers. Central Indian plains in Maharashtra and Nilgiris in southern peninsula also have some rich grasslands. The grasslands of Nilgiris are known as the Shola grasslands.

BirdLife International has reported that 33 globally threatened wetland bird species are found in the wetlands of the Indian subcontinent. The country has innumerable wetlands, which harbour many species of water birds. A few of the most important wetland areas of the subcontinent are Loktak Lake in Manipur, Chilika Lagoon in Orissa, deltaic regions of the rivers Ganges and Brahmaputra, spread over Bangladesh and India, Point Calimere and lake Pulicat in the east coast, Keoladeo Ghana National Park in Rajasthan and Wular Lake in Kashmir. Though Keoladeo is a man-made water body, it has been attracting thousands of water birds, including highly endangered ones like the Siberian Crane, that once used to visit the wetland in good numbers.

The Haor Basin of Sylhet and the flood plains of Mymensingh in the north-east of Bangladesh and wetlands of Indus Valley in Pakistan are some of the other important waterfowl habitats of the subcontinent. Other significant wetlands are the Marine National Park and mudflats of the Rann of Kutch in Gujarat.

Shore birds, waders and sea birds are found throughout the coastal regions of India and Bangladesh. Some of the most important breeding colonies of sea birds are located in Lakshadweep. Deserts and arid regions are some of the preferred areas of birds like the Bustard and Sandgrouse. The most significant desert area, home to a sizable population of birds is the Thar Desert which is situated between India and Pakistan.

THE MYSTERY OF MIGRATION

'Migration' is one of the most interesting and intriguing aspects of the avian world. Birds are forced to migrate to warmer regions during winter. In the warmer months, they return to their original homes. So, migration entails an outward flight from the nesting grounds to resting grounds, known as 'postnuptial' flight and a return flight from the resting area to the nesting area known as 'prenuptial' flight.

Ringing or banding birds is one of the commonest ways to study migration. In fact, scientific banding was first introduced by a Danish ornithologist in 1899 by using zinc bands, which have now been replaced by light aluminium rings. Modern-day technology involves putting satellite transmitters on migratory birds to study them. Migration takes place depending on the climatic conditions and species. Some birds undertake localised migratory movements and follow a very short and specific route, while others do legendary long-distance migration, like Arctic Terns. They migrate from the North Pole to the South Pole and return to the North Pole, which is roughly 10,000 miles. The question that this raises is, do these birds migrate such long distances only for food and nesting or could there be something more to it that we are unaware of?

A pair of Rufous Tree Pies.

Facing page: The Osprey is a migratory raptor.

Pages 42-43: The Coppersmith Barbet can be chanced upon even in big cities.

Before the birds get ready for the long journey, they 'moult'. This keeps the birds in top form as far as their plumage is concerned. They consume enough food and take rest before the migration begins, so that even a small bird like the European Golden Plover can cover a distance of 3,500 km.

Migration of birds of the Indian subcontinent can be classified as extra-limital migration, altitudinal migration, local migration and passage migration. In the subcontinent, most of the migratory birds are winter visitors though there are some birds, which are summer migrants too.

About 160 birds of the subcontinent have been recorded as winter migrants and about 20 birds are summer migrants, such as the Lesser Cuckoo. Other than migratory birds, about 100 species have been recorded as vagrants. The exact figure of the passage migrants is not known, but according to Grimett and Inskipp, it is estimated that there are 19 passage migrants.

Most migratory birds are Ducks, Geese, Waders, Shore birds, Cranes, Swallows, Flycatchers, Thrushes, Chats, Pipits, Wagtails and Buntings. Most birds that migrate into the Indian subcontinent generally breed in central and north Asia, and eastern and northern Europe. Little is known about the migratory routes of birds in north-east Asia. It is thought that the river Brahmaputra and its tributaries form the fly path for birds from north-east Asia. A substantial number of coastal migrants, like the Albatross, travel by oceanic routes. There are some species which breed in East Africa and migrate through Pakistan and north-western India, such as the Rufous-tailed Rock Thrush. It is also believed that many of the migratory birds that come to India and Sri Lanka in winter, fly through Pakistan. The passage migrants generally come from central and northern Asia during winter.

In the Himalayas, altitudinal migration takes place according to seasonal and climatic conditions. During winter, birds of higher altitude descend

A colourful migratory Mallard.

Pages 46-47: Flocks of Demoiselle Cranes over Gujarat Marine National Park.

downwards and return during the summer. The Bar-headed Goose and the Great Crested Grebe breed in summer in high altitude wetlands such as Mansarovar in the Himalayas and come down to the wetlands of the plains in winter. Birds like the Grandala fly up to 18,000 ft in the Himalayas and come down to even 5,000 ft in winter, but never descend to the plains. Local migrants like Openbill Storks and Lesser Whistling Teals, fly shorter distances for nesting and return in winter to the areas from where they had migrated.

The birds in India may be classified into Wetland birds, Tree birds, City birds and Ground birds. We will now look at an enumeration of these various birds on the basis of their habitats.

WETLAND BIRDS

The wetlands of India are distributed throughout the country and harbour a substantial number of birds, of which many are migratory. Some of the most important waterbird areas are Keoladeo Ghana National Park in Rajasthan, Sultanpur Lake in Haryana, Vedanthangal Bird Sanctuary in Tamil Nadu, Ranganathittu Bird Sanctuary in Karnataka, Little Rann of Kutch in Gujarat and Tsomorari Lake in Ladakh.

The Bar-headed Goose migrates to low altitude wetlands in winter.

TREE BIRDS

The largest number of species of birds are tree dwellers. Most of the National Parks and Wildife Sanctuaries hold substantial number of species of tree birds. Raptors are the most important tree-bird species.

The Hornbills are some of the most charismatic birds in the country. They usually prefer dense

Top left: The Plum-headed Parakeet.

Top right: The Lineated Barbet.

Facing page top: The Sapphire-headed Flycatcher.

Facing page bottom left: The Indian Roller.

Facing page bottom right: The Changeable Hawk Eagle.

Top left: The Paradise Flycatcher.

Top right: The Steppe Eagle.

Right: The Rufous-necked Hornbill.

Facing page: The Rufous Sibia.

foliage in forest areas. North-eastern India, eastern India, peninsular India and Andaman and Nicobar Islands are some of the regions where many species of Hornbills can be sighted.

GRASSLANDS AND GROUND BIRDS

Grasslands are amongst the most important bird habitats of the country. Many endangered birds like the Great Indian Bustard, the Bengal Florican, the Koklass Pheasant, the Cheer Pheasant, the Sclater's Monal and the Blood Pheasant are the residents of grasslands. The Himalayan region and the dry and arid thorn forests are among the few good places to observe grasslands and ground birds.

CITY-DWELLERS

Different species of our winged-wonders embrace big cities too. However, how safe is their home in the cities is a question that remains to be answered. The sudden disappearance of the Sparrows from many areas, once a commonly seen city bird, and the near extinction of the Vultures, are but a few cases in point. The list can only be expected to grow longer by the day.

Top left: The Great Indian Bustard.

Left: The Black-hooded Oriole.

Facing page: The Himalayan Bulbul.

CLASSIFICATION OF WILDLIFE

India is a vast country with wildlife as varied as its geographical diversity. Some animals found in different places of the country, such as the Indian Tiger, Indian Elephant, Chital and Sambar to name a few, have the ability to survive in different terrains and climatic conditions. For instance Tigers are found just below the snowline in the Namdapha Tiger Reserve in Arunachal Pradesh, in the mangrove swamps of the Sunderbans in West Bengal and also in the dry and arid regions of Ranthambhore in Rajasthan. This shows that the Tiger has a very high level of adaptability. The Indian Elephant is seen almost throughout the country except the arid zones of Rajasthan. Such is also the case with many other animals that have successfully adapted to their environs.

However, there are some animals, which are found only in particular regions and some that are concentrated only in a few pockets. Here, in this chapter, these animals are categorised under and referred to as 'Regional' and 'Area-Specific'.

REGIONAL

Regionally, the north-eastern states of India are the most important zones in terms of endemic classification. Then comes the peninsular region. It is however impossible to give a complete enumeration of wildlife endemic to different regions of the country, therefore, some out of the many significant species find mention here:

The Hoolock Gibbon (*Bunopithecus hoolock*) is a member of the gibbon family found in India and seen in the north-eastern states like Arunachal Pradesh, Meghalaya and Assam. Male Gibbons are black with distinctive white brows and females and sub-adults are buff. Gibbons swing from tree to tree using their noticeably long arms.

The Lion-tailed Macaque (*Macaca silenus*) is found sporadically across the Western Ghats, from Kerala to Tamil Nadu. It has a black body, white mane and a lion-like tuft at the end of the tail.

The Bonnet Macaque (*Macaca radiata*) is found in the southern peninsula. It is usually slimmer than the Rhesus Macaque and has a longer tail. The hair on the crown is neatly parted.

The Capped Langur (*Trachypithecus pileatus*) is endemic to the north-eastern states, especially

The Clouded Leopard is an arboreal felid and found in the forests of north-eastern India.

Top left: The Bonnet Macaque is found only in peninsular India.

Right: The Lion-tailed Macaque is endemic to the southern peninsular region.

Pages 56-57: Red Panda is found in the evergreen forests of the north-eastern Himalayas.

Arunachal Pradesh, Meghalaya and Assam. From forehead to nape, it is covered by cap-like coarse hair, hence it's name.

The Nilgiri Langur *(Trachypithecus johnii)*, on the other hand, is found in the Western Ghats, from Coorg to Kanyakumari. It is a glossy black monkey with a yellowish-brown head and can be identified easily from a distance.

Once the One-horned Rhinoceros *(Rhinoceros unicornis)* roamed right from the Indus Valley to northern Burma. But due to heavy deforestation and poaching for its horns, it has become region-specific. At present, it is found only in northern parts of West Bengal and Assam. A few Rhinos have been introduced in the Terai region of Dudhwa Tiger Reserve, which is adjacent to the forests of Nepal.

The Rhino prefers to feed on short grass and seeks shelter in thick grasses, which are often 6 m tall. It likes to wallow and remain in water for hours together. Male Rhinoceroses become sexually mature at 10 years of age, but females mature a bit earlier.

The gestation period for a Rhino is 16 months and it usually gives birth to a single calf, rarely two. When born, a Rhino calf weighs about 55 to 60 kg. The lifespan of a Rhino is about 50 years. The Rhino has become endangered due to the

Top left: The Malabar Giant Squirrel is found in the forests of peninsular India, Maharashtra, Madhya Pradesh and Orissa.

Left: The Marbled Cat is also endemic to north-eastern India and its coat resembles that of the Clouded Leopard.

fascination for its horn. It is believed that the horn of a Rhino has high medicinal values and half a kilogram of the same costs about $1000 in Thailand. It is no surprise then that these animals are poached mercilessly.

The Clouded Leopard *(Neofelis nebulosa)* is an arboreal animal, which hunts by night. It is found in the north-eastern parts of India, which include north-west Bengal, Arunachal Pradesh, Meghalaya and Sikkim. It has a distinctly long tail. The colour of its body varies from earthy brown to yellowish brown, fading to pale tawny underparts. The dark blotches lined with black and divided by paler interspaces, give its coat a clouded appearance.

The Marbled Cat *(Pardofelis marmorata)* is also a resident of north-eastern India. It is found in Arunachal Pradesh, Meghalaya, Assam and

The Indian One-horned Rhinoceros seeks shelter in thick grasses and prefers to feed on short grasses.

Sikkim. The coat of this cat has stripes on its crown, neck and back and blotches on the flanks. It is often confused with the Leopard Cat.

The Golden Cat *(Catopuma temmincki)* is another animal endemic to the north-eastern region. It is a resident animal of Arunachal Pradesh, Meghalaya, Assam and Sikkim. It is a stocky cat with a reddish-yellow to golden-yellow coat.

The Spotted Lingsang *(Prionodon pardicolor)* is a member of the Civet family. It also belongs to the north-eastern states, which includes Arunachal Pradesh, Sikkim and Meghalaya. It has a golden coat with large black spots all over its body and has a pointed muzzle.

The Binturong *(Arctictis binturong)* is found in Arunachal Pradesh, Meghalaya, Assam, Sikkim and in the northern part of West Bengal. It looks like a small bear with a shaggy long black coat. The Stripe-necked Mongoose *(Herpestes vitticollis)* is endemic to the Western Ghats. It has a black neck-stripe that reaches backwards from the ear to the shoulder. The colour of its body is grizzled grey. It is the largest of all Asian Mongooses.

The Crab-eating Mongoose *(Herpestes urva)* is a north-eastern species, found in northern West Bengal, Assam, Arunachal Pradesh, Nagaland

The Ruddy Mongoose can be identified by its black-tipped tail.

and Meghalaya. Its dusky coat is coarse and rough. It has a white stripe running from the mouth along each side of the neck and shoulder. Crab-eating Mongooses are more aquatic than other mongooses and they are good swimmers.

The Red Panda *(Ailurus fulgens)* is a habitant of the north-eastern states of India, especially Singalila National Park of northern West Bengal, Namdapha National Park of Arunachal Pradesh and the forests of north Sikkim. It is a bright chestnut-coloured animal with a thick, ringed tail. It has a rounded head with a white face and lower lips.

The Hog Badger *(Arctonyx collaris)* is again a north-eastern species and is found in northern West Bengal, Arunachal Pradesh, Assam, Meghalaya and Sikkim. It has a pig-like snout and bear-like body. It also sports a beautiful grey coat.

The Short-nosed Fruit Bat *(Cynopterus sphinx)* is a habitant of the southern peninsular region. It is a small bat yellowish-grey-brown in colour. Its ears are naked and its divergent nostrils are distinctive.

Both the Black-bearded Tomb Bat *(Taphozous melanopogon)* and the Greater False Vampire Bat *(Megaderma lyra)* are endemic to peninsular India.

The Orange-bellied Himalayan Squirrel *(Dremomys lokriah)* and the Hoary-bellied Himalayan Squirrel *(Callosciurus pygerythrus)* are found in Sikkim, Arunachal Pradesh, Meghalaya, Manipur and Assam in north-eastern India.

The Nilgiri Tahr is found between altitudes of 4,000 ft and 6,000 ft in the Nilgiri hills.

The Nilgiri Tahr *(Hemitragus hylocrius)* is found between altitudes of 4,000 ft to 6,000 ft in the Nilgiris to Annamalai and Western Ghats in southern peninsula. It is a member of India's wild goat family and has a coat that is smoother than that of the Himalayan Tahr.

The Mouse Deer or Indian Chevrotain *(Moschiola meminna)* is endemic to the forests of southern India upto altitudes of 6,000 ft. It is a diminutive deer with an olive-brown skin finely speckled with yellow and three white stripes on the throat.

Area-Specific

There are quite a few species of Indian wildlife, which are area-specific, that is, found in a single forest or in some specific places. Of these, some significant animals are:

The Golden Langur *(Trachypithecus geei)* is endemic to the banks of the river Sankosh in Manas Tiger Reserve in Assam. The rich cream coloured coat of this Langur looks golden in bright sunlight and that makes its black face stand out. The Spectacled Monkey or Phayre's Leaf Monkey *(Trachypithecus phayrei)* is found in the forest of Sipahijola Wildlife Sanctuary in the north-eastern state of Tripura. It is a black-coloured monkey with spectacle-like white rings around both its eyes.

The Asiatic Lion *(Panthera leo persica)*, one of the flagship species of India, is restricted to the Gir National Park in Gujarat. It is a plain tawny-coated animal, with adult males having a mane around

The Asiatic Lion is restricted to the Gir National Park.

their neck. The shade of the mane varies from tawny to brown and is sparser than its African counterpart. The tail has a tuft of hair at the end. Nose to tail, it measures 2.75 m, and weighs between 110 and 190 kg, which is less than the weight of its African counterpart. Indian Lions form a 'pride' with four to five Lionesses, with whom they live. Mainly Deer, Antelopes, domestic cattle and lesser mammals comprise its food. In India, once this majestic cat roamed all over northern India and parts of western and eastern India. But by the end of the 19th century, it is believed that only about 20 Lions existed in the wild. This was due to depletion of their preferred habitats like open grasslands and arid scrub forests and availability of modern fire-arms to the hunters. At present, these are concentrated only in the Gir forests in Gujarat and their population is over 300.

In India, the Pallas's Cat (Otocolobus manul) is found only in Ladakh. It is a small furry cat with a flat head and small rounded ears. This animal is terribly threatened and will be lost forever unless stringent protection measures are taken.

The Marsh Mongoose (Herpestes palustris) is endemic to the wetlands of the southern districts of West Bengal, especially the eastern part of the metropolis of Kolkata. It has a dark coat, pointed snout and dark brown feet.

Bantengs (Bos banteng) were once found in Manipur but their present status is uncertain. A Banteng looks like a reddish-brown ox.

The Mishmi Takin (Budorcas taxicolor taxicolor) is found in the Mishmi Hills, particularly in the Debang Valley district of Arunachal Pradesh.

The Asiatic Wild Ass is found in the Rann of Kutch.

Identified by its wild beast-like horn, the Takin has a big convex face and a very thick neck.

The Chiru or Tibetan Antelope (Pantholops hodgsoni) migrates to the Trans-Himalayan deserts from Tibet. Its colour is fawn on the upper portion and white below, while its face and the stripes down to its legs are black.

The Hangul (Cervus elaphus) is confined only to the Kashmir Valley. The colour of its coat varies from light to dark brown with a broad stripe at the base of its tail. The Hangul has become highly endangered due to poaching.

The Brow-antlered Deer or Thamin (Cervus eldi) is endemic to the Kaibul Lamjao Lake in Manipur and faces serious threat of extinction. Its antlers grow backwards in a long arc and the brow tine

The Brow-antlered Deer or Thamin of Kaibul Lamjao is on the brink of extinction.

is long and noticeable. Due to loss of habitat and mindless poaching, this creature has become highly endangered. Sadly enough, today, only a small population of the Brow-antlered Deer remains in the floating grassland habitat of Kaibul Lamjao wetland, which is also a Ramsar Site. The present number of this Deer could be as low as 85 in the wild. But as it is a prolific breeder, its captive population has done well in the zoological parks, like the National Zoological Gardens in New Delhi and the Zoological Garden in Kolkata.

The Asiatic Wild Ass *(Equus onager)* is a fawn-coloured Donkey with a dark brown fringe on its neck. It is larger than the domestic ass in size and is found in the Little Rann of Kutch in Gujarat. The Asiatic Wild Ass is best seen in the Dhrangadhra Wild Ass Sanctuary. The Tibetan Wild Ass *(Equus kiang)*, on the other hand, is an animal of the Trans-Himalayan cold deserts of eastern Ladakh. It is somewhat larger in size and its reddish-brown colour is deeper than that of its Gujarat counterpart.

Many birds are endemic to the north-east and peninsular India. Some important species of the north-east are: the Wreathed and Rufous-necked Hornbills, the Bengal Floricans, the Assamese Hill Myna.

Important endemic bird species of peninsular India are the Malabar Tree Pie, the Malabar Trogon, the Sri Lankan Frogmouth, the Nilgiri Pipit, among others. Some important endemic birds of the Andaman and Nicobar Islands are: the Andaman Myna, the Nicobar Megapode, the Andaman Parakeet, the Narcondam Hornbill, the Andaman White-bellied Sea Eagle, the Andaman Wood Pigeon and the Nicobar Pigeon.

The Spectacled Macaque is found only in the Sipahijola Wildlife Sanctuary of Tripura.

Extinct and
Endangered Wildlife

T he ecosystem of the earth is a fragile web woven out of a natural system of growth and termination. With the passage of time many animals and plants have become extinct. Species like the Dinosaurs and Mammoths became extinct because they were misfits in the then prevailing natural conditions. But the reasons for the disappearance of animals like the Asiatic Cheetah from India are loss of habitat and indiscriminate hunting. Thus, change in climatic conditions, the theory of survival of the fittest, the rapid march of human civilisation with the forces of industrialisation, a booming human population, exploitation and encroachment of natural resources have taken their toll on the natural resources, wildlife habitats and animal life of India.

The Asiatic Elephant is India's largest land mammal.

At present, the population of India is more than a billion, which is about 15 percent of the total global population. With an increase in the size of the population, exploitation of resources is increasing more than ever. As a result, rapid deforestation is taking place in order to accommodate increased agricultural operations, industrialisation, livestock grazing and the ever increasing development of human habitation.

Technological and industrial progress are directly responsible for unplanned and unlimited exploitation of natural resources like mining inside forested areas, felling of forests for timber, construction of big dams in order to prevent floods and generate limited hydroelectricity—all these practices directly impact animal life. For quicker agricultural growth, pesticides like DDT and Lindane, and chemical fertilisers are used indiscriminately. Besides being harmful for human beings, over-use of these results in discharge of pesticides, toxic chemicals and industrial effluents into water bodies like oceans, rivers, lakes and lagoons. This, in turn, spells havoc for aquatic and marine life, such as Mollusks, Crustaceans, Dolphins, Sharks, Whales, Sea Turtles and thousands of other micro and macro organisms.

Hunting of animals for their meat, skin, bones, tusks and horns or to collect trophies are some other critical factors responsible for depletion of several species in India. Four flagship species namely the Indian Tiger, the Asiatic Lion, the Indian One-horned Rhinoceros and the Asiatic Elephant are now endangered.

One of the most important species of mammals, which has become extinct in India in the last century, is the Asiatic Cheetah (*Acinonyx jubatus venaticus*). An agile hunter, the Cheetah was found in many parts of northern India. Even in the 16th century, Mughal Emperor Jahangir, had more than 200 tamed Cheetahs, which he used

Top right: The Asiatic Lion is one of the prized animal species of India.

Right: The One-horned Rhinoceros is one of the flagship species of Indian wildlife.

Pages 70-71: At present Cheetahs are found only in Africa and Iran.

The Golden Langur is in the endangered list.

for hunting other wild animals. But the entire population of the Asiatic Cheetah has been eliminated due to ruthless hunting and loss of habitat. The One-horned Rhinoceros *(Rhinoceros unicornis)* is another important wild species. It was once found throughout the forests of north and north-eastern India and even in the mangrove swamps of the Sunderbans. Poaching and loss of habitat have been responsible for their depletion. The same factors have propelled the disappearance of at least two bird species. These are the Pink-headed Duck *(Rhodonessa caryophyllacea)* and the Mountain or Himalayan Quail *(Ophrysia superciliosa).* Countless insects, marine life and floral species are becoming extinct everyday due to ignorant and careless use of land and human interference in natural life.

The story is the same for the Indian Tiger and the Asiatic Lion. Earlier, the Indian Tiger was killed for its skin and head as a trophy, but hunting Tigers is no more a mark of bravery. Now the Tiger is killed for its bones and other body parts, which are used in traditional Chinese medicines and drinks, and also smuggled to some of the eastern and south-eastern countries of Asia. In Taiwan, one cup of soup made from the penis of a Tiger may fetch $300, though it has been proven that no body part of the Tiger has any unique medicinal value. To remove such grave misconceptions and myths, it is crucial to build awareness about the utility and importance of each wildlife species on this planet, apart from forming more stringent laws banning poaching and killing.

In India, in the 19th century, Asiatic Lions *(Panthera leo persica)* were found in many parts of northern, western and central India up to the

The Brown Bear's survival is threatened.

river Narmada. Now, it is confined only to the Gir forest of Gujarat. In 1907, the population of Asiatic Lions came down drastically. Due to complete protection provided by the Nawab of Junagarh and currently by the forest department, the number of lions has increased to more than 300.

The Indian One-horned Rhinoceros is killed mainly for its horn, that is rumoured to have medicinal value. At present, it is confined to the state of Assam and northern West Bengal. In 1904, the number of Indian One-horned Rhinoceroses came down drastically. However, after consistent conservation efforts, the number has increased to over 1,500.

The number of Asiatic Elephants in the forests of India, though larger compared to the other three flagship species, is also facing severe threat, primarily due to loss of habitat. Elephants are nomadic by nature and move from forest to forest in search of fodder in large herds, for which they

Bantengs are now almost on the verge of extinction.

Facing page: The Clouded Leopard is one of the rarest cats in India.

use 'forest corridors'. Due to human pressure and unwise land-use, these corridors are being destroyed, resulting in man-animal conflict.

Besides these four animals, many other wild animals and birds are also facing the threat of extinction. Of the 19 primates, 12 are endangered, of which the most critical is the Lion-tailed Monkey. The Pig-tailed, Stump-tailed and Spectacled Macaques, as well as the Golden Langurs are in the 'vulnerable' list. Both the Slender and Slow Lorises are endangered among the Loridae family. In the Ursidae family, the Malayan Sun Bear and the Himalayan Brown Bear are endangered. The Binturong and Spotted Lingsang are facing threat in the Viverridae family. Other than the Jungle Cat, all members of the Felidae family are in trouble, specially the Snow and Clouded Leopards, the Pallas's, Rusty-spotted, Marbled and Golden Cats. Among the

Cervidae family, the Brown-antlered Deer of Manipur, the Hangul of Kashmir, the Hard-ground Barasinga of Kanha Tiger Reserve in Madhya Pradesh and the Musk Deer of the Himalayas are faced with the threat of extinction. Two highly endangered members of the Suidae family are the Pygmy Hog of Assam and the Andaman Hog. Three members of the Bovidae family—the Takin, the Nayan and the Shapu are highly endangered. Another member of this family is the Banteng (a type of ox), which is almost on the verge of extinction. Feral Horses of different colours, which are similar in appearance and nature to North American Mustangs, are found in the Dibrusikhya Wildlife Sanctuary, located close to Dibrugarh town in Assam.

The list of endangered birds is far longer. Some of the endangered birds are: the Great Indian Bustard, the Jerdon's Courser, the Lesser Florican, the Sri Lankan Frogmouth, the Goliath Heron, the White-bellied Heron, the Rufous-necked Hornbill, the Western Tragopan, the Koklass Pheasant, the Sclator's Monal, among many others. In recent times, Vultures, especially the White-rumped, the Long-billed and the

Slender-billed Vultures are facing extinction due to the rampant use of the Diclofenac drug (now officially banned) on cattles as Vultures generally feed on the carcasses of cattle.

Among the herpeto-fauna, the Batagur Baska Turtle, the Leather-backed, Green and Hawksbill Sea Turtles are endangered. All the three types of Crocodiles, namely, the Estuarine, the Gharial and the Marsh Crocodiles are in the endangered list. Among snakes, the King Cobra and the Reticulated Pythons are highly vulnerable. Endangered amphibians include the Himalayan Salamander, also known as the 'Living Fossil', the Malabar Tree Toad and the Garo Hills Tree Toad. Among the marine species, Whales, Sharks, all kind of Rays, the Gangetic Dolphin, varieties of corals, the Horse-shoe Crabs and many others are endangered. In order to prioritise protection of endangered animals in India, the Wildlife (Protection) Act, 1972, has classified different animals and birds into different schedules.

The most endangered animals have been slotted under Schedule I and II of the Wildlife (Protection) Act.

Top: Estuarine Crocodiles are
sometimes more than 22 ft in length.

Right: The Himalayan Salamander, also
known as the 'Living Fossil' is in the
endangered list.

HOME IN THE WILD

Indian forests nurture as many as 14 different kinds of vegetation, each possessing its own peculiar characteristics. Two factors primarily determine the forest type: the rainfall and the altitude. Many National Parks, Wildlife Sanctuaries, Biosphere Reserves, Tiger Reserves, and World Heritage Sites are distributed all over India. Forests and wildlife habitats of India may be classified in groups like the Tropical, the Sub-tropical, the Temperate, the Alpine, and the Fresh Water lakes and swamps. These groups may be further sub-divided. The major forest types, Sanctuaries, Tiger Reserves, and National Parks of India—homes to our diverse wildlife, are discussed in the following pages.

TROPICAL FORESTS

Tropical Wet Evergreen Forest

This type of forest is found where typically the annual rainfall is more than 250 cm. The region remains devoid of rains for about two to three months in a year. This gives rise to dense forests with a tall canopy, which is sometimes higher than 45 m. No individual species is predominant. The major species of trees are the *Dipterocarpus*, the *Actocarpus*, the *Mesua*, the *Hopea* and the *Dysoxylum*. Tropical wet evergreen forests are found all along the Western Ghats covering parts of Tamil Nadu, Karnataka, Kerala, Submontane West Bengal, Orissa, north-eastern states of India and the Andaman and Nicobar Islands.

Semi-Evergreen Forest

This forest-type develops in areas where rainfall is less than 200 cm. This type of forest is a

Top left: Evergreen forests are found in areas with an annual rainfall of above 250 cm.

Right: An Alpine grassland.

Pages 80-81: Landscape of Namdapha Tiger Reserve.

Thorny vegetation of the desert habitat.

Tropical Dry and Moist Deciduous Forests

mixture of deciduous and evergreen species of vegetation. The forest canopy is not as high as in the wet evergreen forests. The major trees of this forest are the *Artocarpus*, the *Terminalia*, the *Albizzia* and the *Phoeta*. This forest-type is found in the Western Ghats, Upper Assam, the lower slopes of the eastern Himalayas and the Andaman and Nicobar islands.

In dry deciduous forest areas, where the rainfall is about 100 cm, the forest canopy grows upto almost 20 m. On the other hand, in moist deciduous forests, the rainfall is within 150 cm and the forest canopy grows upto 25 m. Predominant tree species are the *Tectona grandis,* the *Shorea robusta*, the *Albizzia*, the *Terminalia*, the *Gmelina* and the *Delbergi*. In dry deciduous forests, other than Teak and Sal, the *Madhuca* and the *Diospyros* are also prominent. Many Wildlife Sanctuaries and National Parks fall under the Tropical group.

Littoral and Mangrove Swamps

The littoral and mangrove swamps mainly consist of evergreen trees of varying density and height. The floral species of these forests are usually associated with wetness and salinity. Some major varieties of trees found here are the *Heritiera* sp., the *Calophylum* sp., the *Excoecaria agallocha*, the *Nypa* sp. and the *Sonneratia apetala*.

These swamps are found along the deltaic belts of the Mahanadi, the Godavari, the Krishna, the Kaveri, the Andaman and Nicobar Islands, and best represented in the Sunderbans, which is situated in the Gangetic delta.

Thorn Forest

It is a forest that has low thorny trees and has a canopy less than 10 m tall. Thorn forests are found in areas with an average rainfall of 25 to 50 cm. The *Prosopis*, the Acacia, the *Calotropis*, the *Salvadora* and the *Euphorbia* are some of the major tree species of this type of forest. This type of arid and desert habitat has fewer but important life forms. Lives, which exist here, have grown accustomed to the harsh and difficult conditions. Due to severe scarcity of rainfall, the temperature shoots up to 130^0 F or 55^0 C.

Top right: A multi-coloured Dragonfly.

Right: The Wreathed Hornbill.

The great Indian desert, also known as the Thar Desert, is spread over Rajasthan and Gujarat. It extends over 7,00,000 sq km. The typical vegetation of the desert is the Phog, which grows in the dunes. Other common trees are the Khair, a hardy tree; the Thor, a juicy shrub; and the Khejra, a medium-sized tree.

Other than Rajasthan, thorn forests are found in Punjab, Gujarat, parts of Uttar Pradesh, Madhya Pradesh and Andhra Pradesh. Some important wildlife areas of Tropical forests are discussed in the following pages.

An Elephant crossing a river in Orang.

ASSAM

Kaziranga National Park

It is one of the well-managed parks of the country. The forest, in some parts, is impenetrable and interspersed with vast grasslands. It is considered the most unspoilt valley of the mighty Brahmaputra. Almost the entire forest gets flooded with water from the Brahmaputra during the monsoons and when the water recedes, the grasslands spring to life, which serve as fodder for the Rhinos, the Wild Buffaloes and the Swamp Deer. It is the last stronghold of the Indian One-horned Rhinoceros. Other key species of the Park are Elephants and Tigers. This

National Park also boasts of rich birdlife and harbours one of the highly endangered species of the country—the Bengal Florican. Rosy Pelicans build nesting colonies here during the monsoons.

The tourist season in this incredible National Park is short because monsoons lead to the flooding of the River Brahmaputra.

Manas Wildlife Sanctuary and Tiger Reserve

This mixed deciduous forest of Assam has wide open glades, which lie partly in the Terai and partly in the Bhabar tracts and continues up to Bhutan in the north. The River Manas and its two tributaries, the Benki and the Hekua meander through the forest apart from the River Sankosh which demarcates the boundary between India and Bhutan.

Manas has been declared a 'World Heritage Site' by UNESCO for its awesome bio-diversity. It harbours many species of wild animals including the Tiger, the Elephant, the Indian One-horned Rhinoceros, the Wild Buffalo and the Capped Langur. One of the most vulnerable and endemic wildlife of this forest

Top left: The Scarlet-fronted Sunbird.

Top right: A Red-billed Leothrix.

is the Golden Langur, which is found on the banks of the Sankosh.

The birdlife of Manas is amazing. Great Hornbills, Indian Pied Hornbills, Malkohas, White-capped Redstarts, Hill Mynas and Indian Lorikeets form the avian life of Manas. Insurgency activities of the last decade had damaged a major part of the forest. However, the Park has now been opened to tourists and is slowly regaining its past glory.

Orang Wildlife Sanctuary

Orang, one of the oldest Sanctuaries of the region, is located in Assam, about 145 km from Guwahati on the northern bank of the mighty Brahmaputra. It is a small Sanctuary, comprising mostly grasslands and some moist deciduous trees. The most important animal of the Sanctuary is the Indian One-horned Rhinoceros and the Elephant. A few Tigers and Leopards are also found here. Other animals include the

Porcupine, the Leopard Cat, the Golden Jackal, the Wild Pig, the Black-naped Hare, the Hog Deer, to name a few. Birdlife includes raptors like the Pallas's Fishing Eagle, the Changeable Hawk Eagle and the Marsh Harrier.

ARUNACHAL PRADESH

Namdapha National Park

Wide varieties of forests are found in Namdapha, ranging from wet evergreen forests in the lower parts to mixed deciduous forests in the upper ridges. The altitude varies from 200 m to 4,500 m. The snow-clad Dapabhum is the highest peak of the Park.

Among the protected areas of South-east Asia, the widest variety of wildlife is found in this forest. Three major rivers drain the forest. The Rivers Deban and Noa-Dihing meet at Deban. This makes the view from the forest rest house, located at Deban, most charming.

Namdapha, perhaps, holds the largest variety of cats. The members of the cat family include the Tiger, the Clouded Leopard, the Snow Leopard, the Fishing Cat, the Leopard Cat, the Marbled Cat and the Golden Cat. Hoolock Gibbons are found throughout the Park and move through the dense foliage of tall trees. As a result of this, while their calls can be heard all over, they are difficult to view. Other interesting animals of the Park are the Slow Loris, the Red Panda, the Binturong and the Spotted Lingsang.

The Hoolock Gibbon.

The Asiatic Elephant, the Takin, the Musk Deer, the Goral and the Gaur are some of the other animals found here.

Namdapha boasts of over 500 species of birds. Colourful birds like the Green Magpie, the Malkoha, different species of Laughing Thrushes, Monal and Kalij Pheasants adorn the forests. Five species of Hornbills—the Indian Pied, the Great Indian, the Common Grey, the Wreathed and the Rufous-necked Hornbills, can be sighted here.

MEGHALAYA

Balphakram Wildlife Sanctuary

A combination of evergreen and mixed deciduous trees stretch across Balphakram Wildlife Sanctuary in the Garo Hills of the north-eastern state of Meghalaya. This 292 sq km forest has rolling hills, steep gorges and rivers.

Wildlife in this Sanctuary includes the Tiger, the Leopard, the Leopard Cat, the Golden Cat, the Elephant, the Gaur, the Capped Langur, the Hoolock Gibbon and the Himalayan Black Bear. Large herds of wild Elephants can be seen moving along the forest roads without

Top right : The Orange-billed Blue Magpie is a common bird of the Himalayan region.

Right: Lichen is a symbiosis of algae and fungi found on tree trunks.

Pages 88-89: Mangroves in Marine National Park.

Gibbons. There are records of Swamp Deer sightings in the lower reaches of the forest. The colourful birdlife of this Sanctuary includes Pheasants, Thrushes and Warblers.

bothering human beings. Among the varieties of bird species, the most important is the Grey Peacock Pheasant.

Siju Pitcher Plant Sanctuary

This is a 5 sq km Sanctuary with mixed deciduous forest, 25 km from Tura town, the headquarters of western Meghalaya. It was declared a Sanctuary in 1979 for its Pitcher plants. The flowers of these plants are best seen between December and March.

MIZORAM

Dampa Tiger Reserve

Moist evergreen forests with vast bamboo tracts cover Dampa Tiger Reserve, situated at the north-western tip of the Mizo Hills. The forest is fed by the River Dhaleswari and its tributaries.

Due to the presence of a sizable Tiger population, this Sanctuary was brought under the umbrella of Project Tiger. Mammals found here comprise Tigers, Leopards, Elephants and Hoolock

SIKKIM

Kangchendzonga National Park

This wet temperate mountain forest rises up to bare rock and snow ranges at higher altitudes. On the west, the Park is surrounded by some high peaks of Nepal and India such as Tent Peak, Nepal Peak, Kabur North, Kabur South and Kangchendzonga itself, which is 8,685 m high. The Zemu Glacier flows into the Rivers Zemu and Teesta in the north. The entire region is immersed in colour when Rhododendron flowers bloom between March and May. During the flowering season, the snow melts and hundreds of species of colourful birds adorn the branches of trees. It is an ideal time to photograph the Monal Pheasant, one of the most spectacular birds in the country.

The Clouded Leopard can be sighted in the higher ridges. Leopards can also be seen in the lower forests. Among many endemic animals of the north-east, the Clouded Leopard, the Red Panda and the Binturong roam in this region. The Bharal, the Serow and the Himalayan Tahr are also found here.

WEST BENGAL

Buxa Tiger Reserve

This mixed deciduous forest of the Duars-Terai, the gateway to north-eastern India, is a vital linking corridor, especially for elephants travelling between West Bengal and Assam to the Manas Sanctuary. The forest mostly consists of Sal trees with rich undergrowth, which forms a shelter for

Leopards are large carnivores found throughout the country.

lesser herbivores. There are also some patches of old Teak plantation without any undergrowth.

Buxa is full of wild animals. One of the key species of the Indian forest, the Elephant, is predominant here. Due to the Elephant's shrinking habitat, man-animal conflicts occur frequently in this region.

There have been reports of Clouded Leopard sightings in this Tiger Reserve. Although Leopards are very common in Buxa, the number of Tigers are quite few. The Gaur, the Sambar

and the Muntjac are found in fair numbers. In recent times, Wild Dogs have also been seen in small packs.

Buxa boasts a very diverse and rich avian life. Here the Great Hornbill and the Indian Pied Hornbill can be seen in almost all parts of the forest. Recently, the presence of the Rufous Hornbill has also been reported from the Jayanti Range of the Park. Migratory birds come to the wetlands of Narathuli and Raidak rivers. Migratory ducks include Margansers, Shovelers, Pintails, Large and Lesser Whistling Ducks and Baer's Pochards.

Jaldapara Wildlife Sanctuary

This Sanctuary lies in the foothills of the Bhutan hills. The forest is moist deciduous with a mosaic of grasslands. The Rhino is the flagship species of the forest. In addition, there are the Elephants, the Leopards, the Hog Deer, the Muntjac, the Chital, the Porcupine, the Sambar and the Gaur. There are many reed birds like the Reed Warbler, the Collared Bushchat, the Long-tailed Shrike and others. The Parrot-bill and the Bengal Florican have also been sighted here.

Mahananda Wildlife Sanctuary

Situated in the Terai region, in the foothills of the eastern Himalayas, is the Mahananda Wildlife Sanctuary. It is located in the Darjeeling district of northern West Bengal. The River

Top right: The Royal Bengal Tiger.

Right: The Clouded Leopard in Buxa Tiger Reserve.

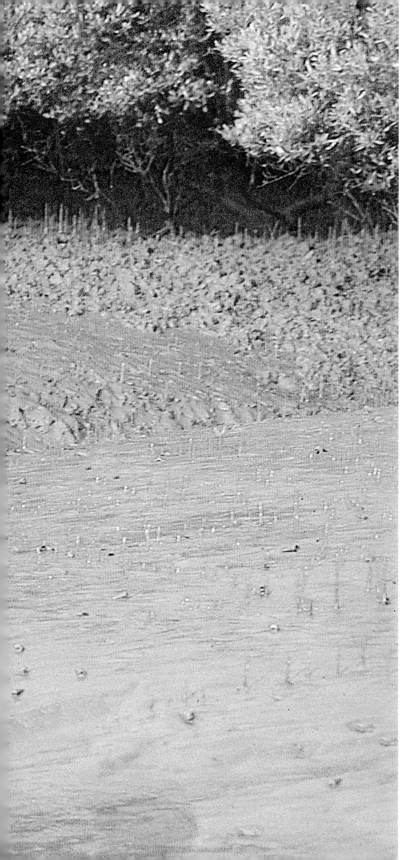

Teesta flows through the eastern flank of the Sanctuary. About 60 percent of this forest is hilly, rising from 150 m to 1,300 m. It is characterised by moderate, steep to precipitous mountain slopes and high ridges towards the north, which gently slope down to almost flat stretches of the Terai and alluvial plains towards the south. The Sanctuary falls in the transition zone between the peninsular Indian sub-region and Indo-Malayan sub-regions of the Oriental region. Mammals found here include the Elephant, the Gaur, the Tiger, the Leopard, the Black Bear, the Assamese Macaque, the Rhesus Macaque, the Himalayan Civet, the Muntjac and the Sambar, to name a few.

Mahananda boasts of a very rich birdlife. The Indian Pied and Great Hornbills, various Flycatchers like the Sapphire Flycatcher, the Little Pied Flycatcher, the Grey-headed Flycatcher, the Leothrix, the Himalayan Tree Pie, the Himalayan Bulbul and many other colourful birds are found here in abundance.

Sunderbans Tiger Reserve

It is the largest deltaic region in the world formed by the tributaries of two great rivers, the Ganga and the Brahmaputra, which flow into the Bay of Bengal. This vast region holds the largest chunk of mangrove forests in the world and this is the only mangrove belt that is an abode of Tigers. Some important rivers that flow through this region apart from the Ganga and Brahmaputra include the Thaukran, the

Due to tidal conditions, catching prey is no easy task for the Tigers of the Sunderbans.

Saptamukhi, the Matla, the Guasaba, the Hogol, the Raimongol, the Jhilla, the Bidya and the Ichamati.

There are 64 species of mangrove trees in the Sunderbans. Some predominant species are the Golpata, the Hental, the Sundari, the Garan, the Bain, the Passur, the Garjan, the Gewa, the Dhundul, the Kankra and the Keora.

The main characteristic of mangrove trees is that they breathe from the air. Hence, they have breathing roots like pneumatophores, stilt roots, knee roots or a perforated bark. The roots also perform the function of holding the river-banks intact.

The Sunderbans are spread across both India and Bangladesh. The Indian part potentially holds a large number of Tigers. Due to tidal conditions, the Sunderbans experience two high tides and two low tides everyday. This makes it quite difficult for Tigers to hunt their usual prey. They prey upon anything that they come across—even crabs and fishes. However, its major prey-base comprises the Chital and the Wild Pig. Other animals include the Rhesus Macaque, the Fishing Cat, the Smooth and the Small-clawed Otters, the Civet, the huge Estuarine Crocodile, the Water Monitor, the Rare Batagur River Terrapin, Olive Ridley Sea Turtle, and the Gangetic and Irawaddy Dolphins.

Sunderban's birdlife is fascinating and varied. Many waders are found in the mudflats which include the Curlew, the Whimbrel, the Common Sandpiper, the Sand Plover, the Common Snipe, the Little Stint, the Redshank, the Greenshank and the Godwit. Seven species of kingfishers—the Black-capped Kingfisher, the Common Kingfisher, the Collared Kingfisher, the Stork-billed Kingfisher, the Pied Kingfisher, the White-throated Kingfisher and the Ruddy Kingfisher are found in these forests. The Goliath Heron, one of the rare birds, is also seen here.

ORISSA

Simlipal National Park

Once a hunting reserve of the maharajas, Simlipal is now a Tiger Reserve. It has one of the finest Sal forests of India. The Mahua, Bahera, Jamun and Wild Mango tree are among the other flora of this region. There are some picturesque falls inside the Park like the Joranda and Baraipani, which cascade into the deep gorges below. The Buriganga and the Khairi River, flow across the forest. Other than the Tiger, the major wild animal of this forest is the Elephant. Tigers are rarely sighted. Elephants are seen roaming in large herds. The Chital, the Sambar and the Wild Pig constitute the major prey-base of the Tigers and the Leopards. Another conspicuous animal of this forest is the Malabar Giant Squirrel.

Indian Pied Hornbills are found in abundance here. One of the main attractions of Simlipal is the Hill Myna. Other important bird species comprise the Jerdon's Chloropsis, the Avadavat, the Golden and the Black-hooded Orioles and the Golden-backed Woodpecker.

Bhitarkanika Wildlife Sanctuary

It is situated in the estuarine region on the confluence of the Rivers Brahmany, Baitarani and the Bay of Bengal. In the mouth of the estuary, there are beaches like Gahirmata and Ekakula, where millions of Olive Ridley Sea Turtles arrive during winter to lay eggs on the sandy beaches. This mass-nesting is known as *aribada*. Recently, the mass-nesting area has largely shifted to another beach nearby called Rashikulya.

Ruddy Kingfisher can be sighted both in Bhitarkanika and the Sunderbans.

Facing page: Collared Kingfishers can be commonly seen in the Sunderbans.

It is primarily a mangrove forest. Sweet water flows through the rivers Brahmany and Baitarani, which help trees grow.

The Chital and hundreds of Estuarine Crocodiles can be viewed here. Egrets, Openbills, White Ibis, Spoonbills, Grey Herons and Cormorants are seen here in good numbers in the rainy season and can be observed till late October. Fiddler Crabs and Mudskippers are found in large numbers on the mud-flats during low tide.

BIHAR

Valmiki Tiger Reserve

Valmiki Tiger Reserve stretches across the northernmost part of the West Champaran district of Bihar, which is a continuation of the Shivalik Range and is contiguous to the Terai of Nepal. The undulating broken tract of the forest with lateretic soil shows high fragile geographical formations, which have resulted in steep ravines, sharp ridges and precipitous walls. The Rivers Gondak and Masan collect water from their numerous tributaries. These rivers and streams keep changing course from place to place, facilitated by the erosion-prone sandy and immature soil of the banks. The Manor, the Bhapsa, the Kapan and the Panchanad are seasonal rivers.

Being essentially a Terai tract, the principal trees of the Park comprise typical trees found in the Terai region. Some important floral species are the *Shorea robusta*, the *Calamus tenuis*, the *Acacia catechu*, the *Dalbergia sisso*, the *Terminalia belarica* and the *Syzygium cumini*.

Though it is a Tiger Reserve, yet the status of Tiger population is not good. Other important mammal species found here include the Leopard, the Fishing Cat, the Leopard Cat, the Chital, the Sambar, the Wild Pig, the Muntjac, the Hog Deer and the Sloth Bear.

This Park is facing a severe crisis due to criminal activities that are going on inside the forest, for example smuggling and felling of Khair and Cane trees.

JHARKHAND

Palamau National Park

Palamau is among the first nine protected areas that were brought under Project Tiger and interestingly, the first ever Tiger census took place in this forest. It is located on the northern edge of the Chotanagpur plateau, and hence has an undulating landscape. It is predominantly a deciduous Sal forest interspersed with trees like the Bahera, the Mahua and the Khair. There are some rich bamboo thickets and grasslands also. The River Koel and its tributaries drain the forest. The ruins of two forts stand on the bank of the River Auranga. The forest has a large number of attractions—majestic Elephants, big herds of Gaur, occasional Leopards and the elusive Tiger, among many other. Other wildlife inhabitants include the Chital, the Sambar, the Wild Pig, the Malabar Gaint Squirrel, the Indian Tree Shrew, the Indian Hare and Porcupines.

Alexandrine, the Rose-ringed and the Plum-headed Parakeets, Purple and Loten's Sunbirds, the Jungle Fowl and the Peafowl, Black-backed and the Golden-backed Woodpeckers, constitute the varied wildlife of this Park. Kamaldih, a beautiful lake inside the forest, attracts Waders and Waterfowls too. Animals are often sighted during dawn and dusk at this pool, especially in summers.

A view of the Koel river-bed in the Palamau Tiger Reserve.

MADHYA PRADESH

Bandhavgarh National Park

Bandhavgarh is one of the most important Tiger Reserves of India. It was originally the private hunting ground of the Maharaja of Rewa. Under his encouragement, the National Park was established in 1968. The forest vegetation

predominantly comprises Sal and Bamboo interspersed with vast grasslands. Other predominant tree species here are the Ber, the Amla, the Bahera, the Jamun and the Mahua. The ruins of a 2,500-year old fort, conquered by different rulers in different periods of time is also located in this Park. A 16 ft long monolithic statue of reclining Lord Vishu is still considered sacred. The place is known as 'Sheshsaya'.

Bandhavgarh is perhaps the best place to see Tigers in India. In sultry summer evenings, Tigers can be viewed from an open jeep from very close quarters. It is possibly one of the best places for researchers to carry out studies on Tigers. Tiger-sighting takes place almost every morning and tourists can see Tigers from elephant-backs. Leopards and Sloth Bears are also not rare here. Occasionally, they can be seen crossing the roads. There are records of Leopard

Cats' presence in Bandhavgarh. Once the Nilgai and the Chinkara were quite common, but now they are rare. A herd of less than 50 Gaurs was seen in Bandhavgarh until 1997. But for some unknown reason, the population shifted to another nearby forest. The Chital, the Common Langur, the Rhesus Macaque, the Sambar and the Wild Pig constitute the primary prey of carnivores in this Park. Wild Dogs are often seen in small packs.

Bandhavgarh harbours raptors like the Crested Serpent Eagle, the Crested Hawk Eagle, the Honey Buzzard, the White-eyed Buzzard, the Lesser Spotted Eagle, the Lesser Kestrel, the Common Kestrel, the Shikra, the Brown Fish Owl, the

Leopards prefer to drag their kill up on the tree tops (Bandhavgarh National Park).

A Peafowl trapped by a Python.

Spotted Owlet and the Barred Owlet. The Peafowl, the Red Jungle Fowl, the Grey Francolin and the Painted Spurfowl are among the ground birds. Tree birds like the Lesser Racket-tailed Drongo, the Black Drongo, the White-bellied Drongo, the Paradise Flycatcher, the Verditer Flycatcher, the Blue-throat, the Ruby-throat, the White-throat, the Chestnut-shouldered Petronia and many others inhabit the Park.

Kanha National Park

Kanha is known as 'Kipling's Country' after Rudyard Kipling who was inspired by this forest to write his immortal *The Jungle Book*. The Mekal mountain range surrounds the southern part of Kanha and in the southern fringe, there is the River Sulkum, which is the main drainage of the valley. Banjar Valley and Halon Valley constitute the western and eastern parts respectively. In recent years, the Supkhar Sanctuary has been merged with Kanha. It is one of the first nine protected areas that was declared a Tiger Reserve.

Kanha National Park and Tiger Reserve are famous for their vast meadows of tall elephant grass, which serve as ideal camouflage for Tigers. The nature of the forest is typically dry-deciduous and the Sal, the Ber, the Mahua, the Flame of the Forest, the Bahera and the thick bamboo groves constitute the primary vegetation of the forest. The Tiger population of this Park is one of the highest in the country and chances of sighting a Tiger in Kanha are very high. Herbivores like

Sub-adult Tigers often climb trees.

Chital and Sambar roam in large herds in these grassy meadows throughout the day.

Kanha is famous for its Hard-ground Barasinga. It is today restricted to this forest, though once it was found in other parts of Madhya Pradesh as well. In the early 70s, the number of Barasingas dwindled to around 50. But due to intensive conservation efforts, the number has reached a viable state. In Bamni Dadar area, which is the highest point of Kanha, the concentration of Gaur is high. Herds of about 30 to 40 Gaurs may be observed at a time. Kanha is perhaps one of the best places to see Wild Dogs. The Wild Pig, the Leopard, the Sloth Bear and the Indian Rattle are among the other wild animals found here. Both the Marsh and Pied Harriers, the Crested Serpent Eagle, the Crested Hawk Eagle and the Honey Buzzard are common raptors found here. Other common birds here include the Plum-headed Parakeet, the Rose-ringed Parakeet, the Peafowl, the Long-tail Nightjar, the Indian Roller and the Red Jungle Fowl.

Top left: The mating ritual of two Tortoise-shell Butterflies.

Top right: The Silk Cotton flower.

Pench Tiger Reserve

Situated in central India's Satpura Range in the state of Madhya Pradesh, this National Park and Tiger Reserve has derived its name from the swift-flowing Pench River that runs from north to south through this Park.

The Park lies within a vast sylvan belt that includes the forest zones of the Seoni, Balaghat and Nagpur districts. The river Pench defines the outer boundary of the Seoni and Chhindwara districts in the Park's upper reaches and forms the state boundary with Maharashtra in the south. The more prominent hills of the Seoni district are known as Arjal Matta, Kalapahad, Chhindimatta and Kumbhadeo. Innumerable seasonal streams of the river Pench criss-cross the forests of the Park. During summers the streams dry up. Myriad perennial natural pools, known locally as *dohs*, serve as waterholes for the Park's fauna. The vegetation of this Tiger Reserve consists of mixed deciduous forest, with Teak (*Tectona grandis*) and Silk Cotton Tree (*Bombax cieba*) being the prevailing species. A great variety of herbs and grasses within the forest sustain the large number of ungulates. Forest products include fruits and flowers of various species, Tendu leaves (rolled to make local cigarette *bidi*), lac (used in the preparation of lacquer), honey and gum.

Sighting Tigers in the Park is usually a matter of chance as they normally avoid people and remain well camouflaged in their dappled environment. Pench is home to a high density of the Wild Pig, the Nilgai, the Chital, the Muntjac, the Chausinga (Four-horned antelope) and the Gaur. The Muntjac can often be spotted under the shaded tree canopies. Frequently seen is the Chinkara (Indian Gazelle), a graceful, slender-built antelope that is light brown in colour. The arched horns sported by males are ringed whereas those of the female are irregular in shape. They inhabitat the open forests, where they feed on cultivated crops, grasses and bushes.

The Park authorities have taken up stringent conservation steps in Pench. The setting up of anti-poaching patrolling camps have greatly contributed to its now flourishing population of wild fauna.

Birdlife of Pench consists of more than 200 species. There are Minivets, Orioles, Barbets, Bulbuls, Wagtails, Munias and Mynas. Common

Kingfishers are abundant by the Pench River. The Marsh Crocodile and freshwater Turtles, such as the Indian Softshell and Indian Roofed Shell are abundant in the Totlah Dam.

Indravati Tiger Reserve

This is one of the larger Tiger Reserves of the country, spread over the four states of Chhattisgarh, Maharashtra, Orissa and Andhra Pradesh. Insurgency has led to tension in the forest. The Sal, the Teak, the Flame of the Forest, the Silk Cotton, the Sissoo, the Arjun, the Mahua and the Jamun are some common trees. The forest has some good thickets of Bamboo as well. This vast deciduous forest is home to Wild Buffaloes, which have become extinct from many other parts of central and northern India. The Tiger is rarely found in this forest. The Leopard, the Striped Hyena, the Golden Jackal, the Sloth Bear, the Gaur, the Chital and the Sambar are also found here.

The River Indravati, which flows through the Tiger Reserve, attracts migratory birds during winters. This is a good place to see Avocets. The Gadwall, the Common Pochard and Lesser Whistling Duck are among the many winter visitors to the Park.

Madhav National Park

On the national highway, passing through Shivpuri, lies Madhav National Park. It was originally the private hunting ground of the Scindias, the maharajas of Gwalior. It has a low hilly terrain, consisting mostly of dry deciduos trees and scrubs. There is a large perennial lake, known as Sakhya Sagar Lake, in the heart of the

Top left: Bonelli's Eagle with a Cattle Egret kill in the Panna Tiger Reserve.

Above left: The Grey Mongoose is common in Panna.

forest. Once there were Tigers found in this forest but sadly, there are none left now. Other wildlife here includes the Nilgai, the Blackbuck, the Sambar, the Chausinga and a few Leopards.

The Sakhya Sagar Lake attracts large varieties of migratory Ducks which include the Lesser Whistling Duck, the Gadwall, the Pintail, the Cotton Teal and the Ruddy Shelduck.

Panna National Park

This tropical dry forest used for hunting by the royal families for ages is now a Tiger Reserve. The topography of the forest is varied in nature. Most of the forest is dry and deciduous. During March-April the trees are leafless. There are rocky gorges in some parts and moist deciduous trees along the banks of the River Ken. The river is the main drainage source of the forest. Though the Tiger population is not very high, the cat can be spotted sometimes.

One of the main attractions of this Park is the diversity of lesser cats. Perhaps, this is one place where one can see Caracals. This elusive animal can sometimes be seen crossing a forest road, especially in summer evenings. The other cats are the Leopard Cat, the Fishing Cat and the Jungle Cat. The main prey of the Tiger are the Chital, the Nilgai, the Sambar, the Chinkara, the Wild Pig and the Chausinga.

Among the birdlife of Panna, the Painted Sandgrouse and the Painted Francolin are the prime attractions.

A Chital Stag in Madhav National Park.

A Sambar doe in the Tadoba Tiger Reserve.

The Peafowl, the Red-vented Bulbul, the Meadow Pipit, the Plum-headed Parakeet, the Rose-ringed Parakeet, the Pied Kingfisher, the White-throated Kingfisher and the Crested Serpent Eagle are the commonly seen birds. Thick-knees and Grey-headed Eagles are found on the banks of the River Ken.

MAHARASHTRA

Tadoba-Andhari National Park

Fortunately, there are still many wildlife refuges in India that stay tucked away from the constant inflow of visitors. One such place is the Tadoba National Park and Tiger Reserve, which retains its unique charm. The Park lies in the Teak belt of central India, which gradually extends into northern Andhra Pradesh. The Park became a Tiger Reserve when it was merged with the adjacent Andhari Wildlife Sanctuary. Its forest consists of mixed deciduous trees encircling the perennial Tadoba Lake. Set amid serene rolling hills, the lake adds in great measures to the Park's tranquil beauty. Besides an abundance of Teak, other interesting tree species here include the Gardenia, the Satinwood, the *Diospyros montano*, the Mahua (Mowra Butter Tree), the Mango and the Jamun (Blackberry). Lofty Jamun trees also encircle the lake; beyond here the ground is marshy till the road. The forest floor is covered with shrubs, and clumps of bamboo are also prevalent.

The Tiger is the prime predator of this forest. The other member of the cat family that is found in Tadoba is the Leopard, which can be seen in late evenings, especially near the lake or fringes of the villages located in and around the Park.

Leopards here feed mainly on stray dogs and domestic Fowl of the villages. The lake attracts many wild animals during dusk and dawn. Wild Dog dens are located in this reserve and sightings of small packs of Wild Dogs are frequent. Palm Civets are common here. The Gaur makes a seasonal appearance at twilight from March to May and the solitary Muntjac is occasionally spotted. The Sambar and the Chital are quite common, the latter roaming in small herds but seen in dozens at twilight. The Sambar feeds on aquatic plants and as darkness sets in, they arrive at the lake to graze. Nilgais number around 300. Wild Pigs, too, are seen in groups of 30 or more. Unlike Chhattisgarh and Andhra Pradesh, the National Parks of Maharashtra do not have Wild Elephants.

The Cattle Egret, commonly found by the lake, are also often seen perched on trees which are at the water's edge. At dusk, they can be seen following Wild Pigs, that roam the lake perimetre in search of insects. The Purple Swamphen and Jacana also make a regular appearance while the Wood Owl and Lesser Owl retreat deep into the forests. Marsh Crocodiles congregate in abundance in the lake waters.

A Russell's Viper glides along the forest floor of Nagzira.

Nagzira Wildlife Sanctuary

Though less publicised, wildlife viewing including Tiger and Leopard sightings is excellent in the Nagzira Wildlife Sanctuary, especially during summer. The forest is a mixed deciduous forest, predominantly with Teak and Sal trees. The Haritaki, the Bahera, the Amla and the Ber are the other flora.

Other than the big cats, large herds of the Gaur, the Chital, the Sambar, the Sloth Bear and the Chausinga roam the forests. Many migratory birds flock to the lake in winter. There are more than 200 species of birds in Nagzira, which include various species of Warblers, Orioles, Flycatchers, Barbets and raptors.

Melghat Tiger Reserve

Melghat lies amidst the tranquil mixed Teak forests in the valley of Gaurilagarh hills in the northern part of Maharashtra, bordering Madhya Pradesh. It is one of the original nine Tiger Reserves of India. The River Tapi drains the forest on the northern fringe. The vegetation is primarily rich dry Teak mixed with other deciduous species like the Mahua (Mowra Butter Tree), the Simal (Silk Cotton Flower), the Bahera, to name a few.

The vegetation and abundance of prey in the Melghat National Park makes it one of the best habitats for the Indian Tiger. About four percent of the dry Vidharba region in the eastern portion

A path through the Valley of Flowers National Park, Uttarakhand.

of the Park comprises Tiger habitat, although in the areas frequented by these regal cats, visitors do not often get to spot them. However, there is generally ample evidence of their presence, such as the remains of a Chital kill or Tiger droppings and pug-marks.

The Gaur is found in good numbers in this National Park. There are small groups of the Chital, the Sambar and the Wild Dog in Melghat. Among birds, Malabar Pied Hornbills are found occasionally. Peafowls, Jungle Fowls, Grey Francolins besides different Warblers are common.

UTTARAKHAND

Corbett National Park

Snuggled in the foothills of the verdant Kumaon mountains is the exotic locale of the Corbett National Park. One of the Premier National Parks of India and the inauguration site of Project Tiger, Corbett lies on the Terai and Bhabar tracts of the Himalayas. In the bygone days of 1935, it was initially known as the Hailey National Park and later renamed in the honour of the famous conservationist Jim Corbett.

It is the first National Park of India. The ink-blue Shivalik ranges of the Himalayan foothills rising in the distance are touched by the mist and golden rays of the sun. The first shaft of sunlight descends obliquely to a shimmering copper rivulet below, where the constant sound of frothing and gushing water breaks the silence of the wild. It was once a hunter's paradise, but is today one of the most fascinating wildlife heritage areas of India.

Top: A view of Ramganga River in Corbett.

Left: A tiny Golden Frog.

Corbett National Park was declared a Tiger Reserve in 1973. The vegetation comprises mixed deciduous forests with Sal, Sissoo, Khair, Amla and other trees. The Tiger Population of Corbett is a healthy number now. Faunal diversity comprises the Elephant, the Leopard, the Chital, the Sambar, the Wild Pig, the Hog Badger and the Muntjac. The Indian Rock Python is occasionally seen basking in the sun. In summer, large herds of Elephants are seen roaming in the grasslands of Dhikala.

The Paradise Flycatcher, the Indian Pitta, the White Eye, Orioles, the Plumbious Redstart, the White-capped Redstart, the Green Malkoha, the Kalij Pheasant and the Green Magpie are among the prominent bird species found here.

Valley of Flowers National Park

As the name itself suggests, Valley of Flowers, situated in the Garhwal ranges of the Himalayas, is one of the most fascinating places of natural beauty in the country. It is part of the Nanda Devi Biosphere Reserve. Hem Kund Sahib, a pilgrimage of the Sikhs, is located within the vicinity of the National Park. The area is famous for its wild flowers. Various wild flowers like the Brahma Kamal, the Blue Poppy, among others, bloom during July-September, which attract hundreds of species of Butterflies. The Himalayan Tahr, the Musk Deer and Leopards are some of the wild animals that can be seen in the region. The Alpine Cough, the Red-billed Blue Magpie, the Eurasian Jay, the Himalayan Griffon, the Plumbous Redstart and the Crimson-breasted Sunbirds are among the birds found in the National Park.

Nanda Devi National Park

A vast and undisturbed stretch of alpine forest lies in the vicinity of the Nanda Devi peak, which is the second highest peak of the country at 7,816 m. Eric Shipton and Bill Tilman were the first two persons to visit the virgin forest. The floral pattern comprises the Rhododendron and the *Betula utilis* in the lower reaches and the Juniper, the Birch, the Fir and the *Picea sp.* in the upper parts of the National Park.

The Bharal, the Goral, the Serow, the Musk Deer and occasional Snow Leopards are among some of the Himalayan animals found within the fascinating landscape of the forest. It is a haven for various Pheasants too. The Monal, the Cheer, the Koklass Pheasants, and the Terminick's Tragopan are inhabitants of the Park. Hundreds of Himalayan tree birds are found in this alpine pasture. The Park has been designated as a Biosphere Reserve.

The Ranthambhore Tiger Reserve with the Ranthambhore Fort in the background.

UTTAR PRADESH

Dudhwa Tiger Reserve

Due to the single-handed efforts of the internationally famed conservationist, Arjan Singh, popularly known as 'Billy', the Terai forest of North Lakhimpur district of Uttar Pradesh, which is within the proximity of the Himalayan foothills, was declared as Dudhwa Wildlife Sanctuary and subsequently designated a National Park and brought under Project Tiger.

There are some lakes and waterbodies inside the Park, namely, the Tigertal, the Banketal and the Jhadital. The forest is a predominantly typical moist and dry deciduous Terai tract of rich Sal (*Shorea robusta*) trees. There are vast savannah grasslands interspersed with forests consisting of the *Terminalia tomentosa*, the *Dalbergia sisso*, the *Terminalia belerica*, the *Acacia catechu* and the *Syzygium cumini*. There is a patch of Eucalyptus trees just near the entrance of the Park.

The Tiger is, no doubt, the most fascinating mammal species of the Park. However, there have been instances of man-tiger conflict in this National Park. Due to proximity to the Palia village and the absence of a buffer zone, there were some incidents of Tigers attacking humans. The Leopard is the other large carnivore of this forest, though the number of Leopards are less compared to Tigers. Some Indian One-horned Rhinoceroses were introduced under the Rhino Re-introduction Scheme in 1985. A few of them have migrated to the adjacent Sukla Phanta forest in Nepal. The number of Rhinos in Dudhwa has increased to about 20.

The Pheasant-tailed Jacana in breeding plummage in Rajbagh Talao, Ranthambhore Tiger Reserve.

The Black Scorpion in Desert National Park.

Other fauna species which are found here include the Wild Pig, the Honey Badger, the Hog Deer, the Muntjac, the Chital, the Indian Red Fox, the Golden Jackal and the highly endangered Hispid Hare. Out of the 350 species of birds available in Dudhwa, the Bengal Florican and Lesser Florican or Leekh are among the highly endangered birds of India. Migratory species include the White-eyed, Red-crested and Common Pochards, Pintails and Mallards. The Indian Rock Python, the Spectacled and Monocled Cobra, the Common and Braided Krait are listed among the reptilian species.

RAJASTHAN

Ranthambhore National Park

Nestled in the valleys of the Aravalli and Vindhya mountain ranges is the pristine forest of Ranthambhore. The region has a strong history associated with it and as a testimony to that, a ruined fort still stands at the entrance of the Park. The predominant tree species are dry deciduous and include the Dhok, the Ronj, the Ber, the Acacia, the Salai, the Date Palm, the Wild Mango, the Peepal and the Banyan.

Ranthambhore is famous for its Tigers. Other than Bandhavgarh and Kanha, no other forest offers such a close view of Tigers. Since the inception of Project Tiger, due to intensive conservation efforts, Tigers have become more and more active during daytime. The Tigers here seem to have lost all fear of humans. Leopards are also not uncommon here and are found on the fringes of the forest. Leopards are often sighted in the Kachida Valley. There have been reports of Caracal sightings. The Hyena, Golden Jackals and Jungle Cats are common carnivores of

this forest. Sloth Bears are found in areas like Lakarda and Anantpura. The Chital, the Sambar, the Nilgai, the Chinkara and the Wild Pig form the major prey of Tigers and Leopards. The Indian Hare, Common and Ruddy Mongooses and Water Monitor Lizards are some of the other animals inhabiting Ranthambhore. Marsh Crocodiles are regularly seen on the banks of the Rajbagh Talao and Padam Talao. The Park holds a good population of raptors like the Crested Serpent Eagle, the Honey Buzzard, the Shikra, the Bonelli's Eagle, the Pallas's Fishing Eagle and the Marsh Harrier. The Painted Sandgrouse, the Painted Spurfowl and the Painted Francolin are a photographers' delight.

Various wading birds like the Black-winged Stilt, the Bronze-winged Jacana, the Pheasant-tailed Jacana, the Greater Thick-knee are found near the waterbodies.

Sariska Tiger Reserve

This dry deciduous pocket of forest lies at the foothills of the Aravallis. Being dry deciduous in nature, the vegetation of this Tiger Reserve comprises mainly of the Acacia, the Ber, the Dhok, the Surwal, the Tendu and Goria. Though Tiger sighting was quite frequent here, Sariska has lost its glory in recent years due to heavy poaching of Tigers. The entire Tiger population has been wiped out. There is a plan to reintroduce Tigers in this Reserve. Among other animals, there are plenty of Nilgai, Chital, Sambar

Top left: Green-whip Snake.

Left: The Nephila Spider weaving a web.

A Lioness in Gir.

and Wild Pig. The Common Peafowl, the Grey Partridge, the Bush Quail, the Painted Sandgrouse, the Painted Spurfowl, the Crested Bunting, the Meadow Pipit and many others constitute the avian life of the forest.

Desert National Park

In close proximity to the historical town of Jaisalmer lies the Desert National Park. Most of the area around it still holds the status of a Sanctuary. The nature of the flora is typically desert-like. Much of the area is covered with shrubs, cacti and even some trees. Some places have sand dunes. There are the villages of the Bishnois, who are the traditional protectors of desert animals. Wildlife of the area constitute the Blackbuck, the Chinkara, the Grey Wolf, the Desert Fox, the Desert Cat and the Indian Hare. Birdlife comprises the Short-toed Eagle, the Tawny Eagle, the Laggar Falcon, the Spotted Eagle, the Kestrel and the Grey Francolin.

GUJARAT

Gir National Park

The last foothold of the Asiatic Lion is the Gir National Park, situated in the south-western part of Saurashtra in Gujarat. It is a dry and mixed deciduous forest consisting of Teak, Flame of the Forest, Acacia, Jamun and occasional Banyan trees.

It is believed that in 1913 only about 20 Asiatic Lions were left in Gir and were on the verge of extinction. But after prolonged and intensive conservation efforts, the number has now increased to about 300. Other wildlife here include the Chital, the Sambar, the Chausinga, the Chinkara, the Wild Pig, the Common Langur, the Hyena and the Golden Jackal. Gir boasts of a rich birdlife of the arid regions. The Sandgrouse is a common bird here. Other birds include the Crested Lark, the Crested Bunting, the Peafowl, the Red Jungle Fowl, the Grey Francolin, the Bush Quail, the Shaheen Falcon,

Top left: The Indian Porcupine in Bandhavgarh.

Top right: A Painted Sandgrouse in Gir.

the Brown Fish Owl, the Bonelli's Eagle, to name a few.

In Kamaleswahri Dam, Marsh Crocodiles are spotted regularly and a Crocodile breeding farm has been established at Sasan. The Indian Rock Python is also found here.

Dhrangadhra Sanctuary

It is the only Asiatic Wild Ass Sanctuary of the country, located in the Little Rann of Kutch. The Rann is a vast hard saline mudflat along the India-Pakistan international border with very little vegetation. The Wild Asses migrate freely between the two countries.

One of the highly endangered birds of India, the Great Indian Bustard, is an attraction of this region.

TAMIL NADU

Mudumalai Wildlife Sanctuary

It is a mixed deciduous forest lying on the Western Ghats. It is connected with Bandipur Tiger Reserve in Karnataka and Wynad Wildlife Sanctuary in Kerala.

The Sri Lankan Frogmouth is a rare bird.

The River Moyar forms the boundary between Mudumalai and Bandipur and provides drainage to the entire region. It is a dense forest with vast grasslands in Masinagudi. The animals of the forest move freely between Bandipur and

Ornamental Star Tortoises are victims of illegal trade.

Annamalai Wildlife Sanctuary

This mixed deciduous forest with predominantly Rosewood and Teak trees lies between the northern-end of the Cardamom Hills of Kerala. The moist parts of the forest are full of Leeches. The focal point of the Sanctuary is known as the Top Slip. The river Sricaippallam drains the Sanctuary. Herds of Elephants are found on the banks of the river. The evergreen Shola forest provides a secure shelter for Lion-tailed Macaques and Nilgiri Langurs.

The Mouse Deer, the Chital and the Sambar are also found here. The birdlife of the region comprises many colourful Malabar birds.

Kalakad Mudenthurai Tiger Reserve

Kalakad Mudenthurai is a perfect example of a rain forest. Trees here are lofty with their buttressed boles attracting botanists. The River Tambrapari drains the Tiger Reserve. Tigers in this Reserve are nocturnal by nature and therefore hardly seen during day time. The Lion-tailed Macaque, the Nilgiri Langur, the Nilgiri Tahr and Malabar Giant Squirrel are the prime wild attractions. Among some interesting birds of the area are the Malabar Trogon, the Malabar Hornbill and Malabar Thrush.

Vedanthangal Sanctuary

Close to the Chennai city, lies a beautiful small lake surrounded by lush greenery, which has been declared a Sanctuary called the Vedanthangal Sanctuary. Many resident birds as well as migratory waterfowl are found around this lake region.

Mudumalai. Large herds of Elephants are seen on the banks of the River Moyar during summers. Tigers are also sighted occasionally. Gaurs are found in large scattered groups. The Kargudi area is known to have a good Leopard population. Another important predator, the Wild Dog is seen roaming around in packs in the Sanctuary. Other ungulates commonly seen here include the Chital and the Sambar.

Mudumalai enjoys an extensive birdlife. Mynas and Rose-ringed Parakeets are found in flocks. Orioles and Barbets are common. Among raptors, the Crested Hawk Eagle and the Crested Serpent Eagle are found in abundance. Collared and Oriental Scops Owls, the Spotted Owlet, the Brown Fish Owl, the Malabar Trogon, the Malabar Grey Hornbill, the Malabar Pied Hornbill and Malabar Great Black Woodpecker are among the varied birdlife, which adds colour to this forest.

KARNATAKA

Bandipur National Park

This National Park is also a Tiger Reserve. It is bound by Nagarhole, Wynad and Mudumalai on the north-west, west and south respectively. The forest of Bandipur is not very dense. Elephant herds spend almost entire days on the banks of the River Kabini, which divides Bandipur from Nagarhole, and large families of Elephants are often seen moving around and even playing in the forests. Herds of Gaurs can be seen throughout the forests.

Tigers are rarely seen here, though it is a Project Tiger Reserve. The Chital, the Muntjac, the Wild Pig and the Malabar Giant Squirrel comprise the other wild animals residing in the Park. The Red-whiskered Bulbul, the Malabar Tree Pie, the Malabar Grey and Great Hornbills are also seen perched on trees here.

Bhadra Tiger Reserve

The moist deciduous forest of Karnataka is now a Tiger Reserve. The forest is located in the Bhadra River Valley, which is encircled by the Bababudan Range. Though it is a Tiger Reserve, the Tiger is elusive and rarely seen here. The Reserve enjoys a large Gaur population. Elephants are also occasionally sighted. Other animals that reside in this forest include the Chital, the Sambar and the Ruddy Mongoose. Birdlife here includes some of the Malabar species.

Facing page: A Malabar Pied Hornbill.

Nagarhole National Park

It is considered to be one of the few forests of peninsular India where wildlife can be observed easily from close quarters. It lies on the northern bank of the River Kabini with tall bamboo groves and wide grassy expanses, which stretch between the Western Ghats and the Nilgiri mountains. The upper canopy of the forest has some valuable timber trees such as the Mathi, the Nandi, the Hone and Tadasalu. The forest is home to two very expensive varieties of trees, namely, the Rosewood and the high-quality Teak. In the lower reaches, there are the Nelli, the Kooli, the Kadu Tega, the Flame of the Forest, the Kakke and Bamboo. Nagarhole has over 1,200 wild Elephants. Elephants are usually migratory by nature. During winter, when forage is abundant, they stay scattered. But during summer, when there is scarcity of forage as well as water, all assemble on the banks of the Rivers Mulehole and Kabini. Gaurs are often found in herds of 20 to 25 grazing lazily. Karapura is one of the ideal places to see Leopards, specially at dusk. The Chital and the Sambar are also found in abundance.

Occasional Tiger sightings are not uncommon in this Park. Other animals include the Chausinga, the Muntjac, the Wild Pig, the Black-naped Hare, the Indian Porcupine, the Wild Dog, as well as the elusive Mouse Deer. The secretive Slender Loris and Flying Squirrels are also found in this unique National Park. Marsh Crocodiles and Water Monitors are seen lazing on the river Kabini occasionally.

Nagarhole has an immense variety of avian life. Among raptors are the Grey-headed Fishing Eagle,

Smooth-coated Otters frolicking in the River Periyar.

the Osprey, the Crested Hawk Eagle, the Shaheen Falcon, the Crested Serpent Eagle, the Indian Hobby, the Red-headed Vulture and the Honey Buzzard. The Grey Jungle Fowl, the Peafowl and Red Spurfowl are common.

The Malabar Pied Hornbill, the Malabar Black Woodpecker, the Malabar Trogon, the Yellow-legged Green Pigeon, the Malabar Whistling Thrush, the Hill Myna, the Scarlet Minivet and the Paradise Flycatcher are among the other birds which have made this Park their home.

KERALA

Eravikulam National Park

This Shola forest has a wide expanse of undulating grasslands and emerald forests amidst valleys. The highest peak of South India, Anaimudi, is located here.

The Nilgiri Tahr is one of the main attractions of the region. They can be normally spotted near the Rajamali Tea Estate. Other wildlife consists of the Elephant, the Leopard, the Nilgiri Langur, the Lion-tailed Macaque and the Malabar Giant Squirrel.

Periyar National Park

Some spectacular patches of mixed forest types exist around the 55 sq km dam on the river Periyar. While constructing the dam, a big portion of the rich forest had been destroyed. The black stumps of the dead trees still jut out of the water adding an eerie beauty to the park.

It is a Tiger Reserve. There are vast and open grasslands and semi-evergreen patches like the *Terminalia,* Teak and Sholas. In fact, these are tropical evergreen forests, where trees run up to the height of 100 ft to 130 ft. In some parts, the dense tree canopy does not allow even sunrays to penetrate. Due to the damp climate, there is rampant growth of reeds, climbers, ferns and Orchids. Most of the places are full of leeches and it is advisable to enter the forest with leech-guards. The best place to observe wildlife in the wilderness here is Manakavla, which is a 3 km trek.

Herds of Elephants can be seen grazing in the green valley during one's boat ride on the lake. Smooth-coated Otters are found in the lake water. Among the Deer species, there are the Muntjac, the Sambar and Mouse Deer. Bonnet Macaques are found all over. Malabar Giant Squirrels, Nilgiri Langurs and Flying Squirrels are seen perched on trees. Manakavla is an ideal place to see Wild Dogs and Wild Pigs. Chances of sighting the Tiger are, however, poor.

On the rocky shore along the lake, Monitor Lizards are often spotted. Pythons and King Cobras are also found here. The River Periyar is known to harbour Flying Snakes, Flying Lizards and Flying Frogs. Malabar Hornbills, Grey Hornbills, Ospreys, Malabar Trogons, Malabar Pipits, Malabar Tree Pies, Malabar Thrushes and Fairy Blue Birds are common here.

Silent Valley National Park

The Silent Valley is peninsular India's last virgin primary tropical forest. It is a nursery of some rare herbs and plants and a wonderland for botanists. Elephants, Lion-tailed Macaques and Tigers are among the wildlife found in the region.

ANDHRA PRADESH

Nagarjunasagar Tiger Reserve

Nagarjunasagar-Srisailam, one of the largest Tiger Reserves of the country, lies among the rugged terrain with meandering gorges cut by the River Krishna through the Nallamalai hills of central India. It is primarily a dry deciduous forest consisting of scrubs and bamboo groves. The predominant flora of the region are the Teak, the Redwood, the Kendu and the Haldu.

The Tiger Reserve is rich in ungulate diversity. The Blackbuck, the Chinkara, the Chausinga and the Nilgai are among the Antelopes found within the Park. Among the Deer species, there are the Chital, the Sambar and the Muntjac. Tigers are usually elusive. The Golden Jackal, the Fox, the Honey Badger and the Malabar Giant Squirrel are not very difficult to see. Marsh Crocodiles are found lazing in the Krishna River. The Malabar Hornbill, the Malabar Tree Pie, the Fairy Blue Bird, the Crested Lark and the Grey Francolin are common in this Tiger Reserve.

SUB-TROPICAL FORESTS

Sub-Tropical Broad-leaved Hill and Pine Forests

Broad-leaved forests are found between altitudes of 1,000 and 1,700 m. These type of forests thrive in areas where rainfall varies between 75 to 125 cm. Pine forests receive an annual rainfall of 150 cm to 300 cm. Broad-leaved hill forests are generally evergreen high forests where the *Calophyllum*, the *Cinnamonum*, the *Castanopsis*, the *Shima* and *Michelia* comprise some of the major flora.

In Pine forests, two species of Pines, namely, the *Pinus roxburghii* and the *Pinus insularis* are the two dominant ones. Broad-leaved hill forests occur in the Nilgiris in south India, central India, Bihar, West Bengal and north-eastern states. On the other hand, Pine forests feature in Uttarakhand, Assam and along the western and central Himalayas.

TEMPERATE GROUP

Montane Wet Temperate Forest

This is an evergreen forest without Conifers. Normally such forests are found at an altitude of 1,500 m. The *Temstroemia*, the *Michelia*, the *Quercus*, the *Acer* and the *Machilus* are the major floral species available here.

Wet temperate forests are seen in the Nilgiris, the Annamalai and Tirunelvelli hills in

Rhododendron blooms in April in the western Himalayas.

peninsular India and in the eastern Himalayas in West Bengal, Assam and Arunachal Pradesh.

HIMALAYAN MOIST TEMPERATE FOREST

Himalayan moist evergreen forests are found between altitudes of 1,600 and 3,500 m. Oaks and Conifers are predominant here. The major flora comprises the *Cedrus deodora*, the *Abies pindrow*, the *Quercus* sp., and the *Picea smithiana*. Moist temperate forests are found in the western Himalayas in Jammu and Kashmir, Himachal Pradesh and Uttarakhand and in the eastern Himalayas in the Darjeeling district of West Bengal and Sikkim.

The Sacred Brahma Kamal in the Valley of Flowers National Park in Uttarakhand.

Facing page: A view of the Chaukhamba Peak from Chandrashila in the western Himalayas.

HIMALAYAN DRY TEMPERATE FOREST

These types of forests are characterised by predominantly Conifer species. The major trees are the *Pinus wallichiana*, the *Pinus gerardiana*, the *Quercus ilex*, the *Pinus wallichiana* and the *Betula* sp. Such forests are found in Jammu and Kashmir, Punjab, Himachal Pradesh, Uttarakhand and parts of the north-eastern states. Some important wildlife areas of temperate forests are:

HIMACHAL PRADESH

Great Himalayan National Park

In Kulu district of Himachal Pradesh, the Great Himalayan National Park lies amidst the snow-clad western Himalayas. The Park is drained by the rivers Jiwa, Sainj and Tirthan, all of which flow westwards into the River Beas. The Oak, the Juniper, the Silver Fir and the Blue Pine comprise the principal flora of the forest. It is the abode of the Bharal (Blue Sheep), the Musk Deer, the Muntjac, the Himalayan Brown Bear, the Leopard, the Common Langur and the Rhesus Macaque. The Park is home to a variety of Pheasants, including the Cheer Pheasant, the Monal Pheasant, the Koklass Pheasant and the Kalij Pheasant.

JAMMU & KASHMIR

Dachigam National Park

Dachigam is located 22 km from the state capital, Srinagar. Dachigam can be divided into

A delicate abode of the Plain Tiger Butterfly.

Facing page top: The Koklass Pheasant.

Facing page bottom: An Alpine forest.

two sectors: Upper Dachigam and Lower Dachigam. The picturesque River Dagwan flows across Lower Dachigam and forms the famous Dal Lake in Srinagar. Trees like the Mulberry, the Willow and the Oak are the predominant species with thick and dense undergrowth in the lower reaches. The upper reaches lie on the eastern flank, comprising two-thirds of the entire area. Juniper, Birch and Blue Pine trees are predominant in Upper Dachigam.

The prime attraction of Dachigam is its Hangul Deer, which may be considered a cousin of the Red Deer of Europe. The species is endemic to Kashmir and in recent years has become critically endangered. The best time to see Hangul herds is at the onset of winter, when the upper reaches are covered with thick snow and the animals descend to the lower reaches.

Another important animal of Dachigam is the Brown Bear, which is also endangered. Different species of Marmots and Martins, the Markhor, the Musk Deer and Leopards are among the other animals found here.

The Monal Pheasant, the Blood Pheasant and the Koklass Pheasant, the Yellow-billed Blue Magpie and the Lammergeier are some of the spectacular birds found in the region.

ALPINE FOREST

Alpine forests occur in the Himalayas, above the timber limit. Temperatures remain below freezing point almost throughout the year. In alpine forests, high trees are replaced by scrubs, which vary in form according to the moisture supply in different months.

The major trees here are the *Picea smithiana*, the *Abies sp.*, the *Betula utilis*, the *Rhododendron camanulatum*, the *Juniperus cummunis*, the *Juniperus recurva* to name a few.

Hemis High Altitude National Park

The National Park covers the Martho and Rumbak valleys. In most places, the rock-face is exposed and trees are sparse. Only some Juniper, Birch and Blue Pine are found. The Bharal, the Ibex and the Snow Leopard are some of the endangered animals of the region. The birdlife consists of the Snow Partridge, the Snow Pigeon, the Monal and other high-altitude species of birds.

WETLANDS

Wetlands and water bodies are those significant wildlife habitats that attract a number of migratory as well as resident Ducks, Waders, Storks, Cranes and Kingfishers. Wetlands may be classified into two categories—wetlands of upper ridges and wetlands of the plains. Some of the water bodies have been declared as Ramsar Sites, which have made them wetlands of international importance. Some of these are Loktak Lake, Wular Lake, Hariake Lake and Keoladeo Ghana National Park.

Wetlands of Upper Ridges

There are some places in Uttarakhand, like Kakragad, 35 km from Rudraprayag, located on

The tall woodlands of the eastern Himalayas.

the banks of the River Mandakini, that give rise to many small pockets of wetlands.

These pockets attract hundreds of Himalayan species like the Forktail, the Brown Dipper, the Blue Whistling Thrush, and the Himalayan Bulbul, among others. The banks of River Mandakini itself attract many birds, such as the Himalayan Kingfisher and the Himalayan Griffon to name a few. Another such wetland, Deoriatal, from where the Chaukhamba Peak is quite close, attracts many Himalayan birds like the Snow Partridge, the Streaked Laughing Thrush, the Yuhina, the Grey-winged Black Bird, the Grosbeak and many others. The Mansarovar Lake is another important bird area. The Brahminy Duck breeds in this lake.

The Tsomorari Lake is located in the state of Jammu and Kashmir. It is situated at an altitude of 15,200 ft above sea level, 230 km away from Leh. It takes fives days to trek around the lake. It is the breeding ground of the Bar-headed Geese, the Mergansers and the Great Crested Grebes.

Wetlands of Plains

There are thousands of small, medium-sized and large wetlands scattered throughout the plains in the country. These attract many migratory birds, waders and animals. Some of the most important wetlands are mentioned here.

The Yellow Bittern foraging in the swamps.

RAJASTHAN

Keoladeo Ghana National Park

Keoladeo Ghana in Bharatpur was originally developed by a maharaja for the purpose of hunting Wild Fowl in the late 19th century. It was named after a temple located inside the Park. There are several lakes which are fed entirely by rain as well as by water of the Rivers Gambhir and Banganga through a canal. The Park contains 181 genera and more than 220 species and sub-species of trees.

The predominant species here is the Babool. Other species constitute the Ber, the Kalam, the Khajur and the Khejri. The wetlands contain large number of weeds and acquatic plants. The lakes are full of Snakes, Frogs, Leeches, Turtles and fishes including large Cat Fishes. Mammals like the Chital, the Sambar, the Wild Pig, the Nilgai, the Rhesus Macaque and the Golden Jackal are quite common here. Keoladeo is a paradise for ornithologists and bird watchers. During monsoons, large heronries are formed in this Park. These birds include Painted Storks, Openbills, Spoonbills, White Ibises, Large, Median and Little Egrets, Cormorants and Shags. Waders include the Indian and the Purple Swamphens, the Pheasant-tailed Jacana, the Bronze-winged Jacana, the Common Sandpiper, the Snipe and the Black-winged Stilt.

Winter is the season for arrival of migratory Ducks such as the Gadwall, the Pintail, the Shoveler, the Spot-billed Duck, the Mallard, the Common Pochard, the Common Teal and Red-crested Pochard. Hundreds of tree-birds are found throughout the year. These birds include

A nesting Indian River Tern.

the Baya Weaver Bird, the Black-headed Myna, the Purple and Loten's Sunbird, the Drongo and many others.

MANIPUR

Kaibul Lamjao National Park

This floating forest of north-east India is the last foothold of the highly endangered Sangai, which is famous as the Brow-antlered Deer. The floating vegetation area here is known as Phumdi. Though the Park is 36 sq km in size, the Sangai is found only within 6 sq km. At present, there are more Sangais in the zoological parks of India than in the wild. The Delhi National Zoo and Kolkata Zoological Garden are the places where captive breeding of Sangais has been carried out quite successfully. Other wild animals found in this National Park

include the Fishing Cat, the Hog Deer and Wild Pig. Some migratory Waterfowl are also seen during winter.

KARNATAKA

Ranganathittu Bird Sanctuary

On the north of Mysore city, near Tipu Sultan's capital Srirangapatnam lies Ranganathittu, spread across small islands of the River Cauvery. Heronry begins in early June. Nesting birds consist of the White Ibis, the Median, Large and Small Egrets, the Cormorant, the Spoonbill, to name a few. Baya Weavers and River Terns are seen nesting in early July. A close view of the nests is possible from boats. Marsh Crocodiles are an added attraction.

TAMILNADU

Vedanthangal Sanctuary

This is a very small Sanctuary with trees growing in and around a small village pond. The area is protected by law since 1798 and shooting is prohibited. Migrant Ducks arrive here during winter. Many species of breeding Waterfowls are found here.

MARINE LIFE

India is surrounded by sea in the east, west and south. The sea waters are home to an abundance

A view of Chaukhamba Peak from Deoriatal in Garhwal Himalayas.

of rich marine life. Andaman and Nicobar Islands, Lakshadweep, Gulf of Mannar, Point Calimere and Gujarat coasts are highly rich in marine life and in bio-diversity. Many species of edible fishes and shell fishes like the Gray Mullet (*Mugil cephalus*), the Indian Salmon (*Polynemus indicus*), the Bhetki (*Lates calcarifer*), the Tiger Prawn (*Penaeus mondon*) and the White Prawn are found here. Innumerable ornamental fishes, large coral reefs, colourful sponges, curious-looking Nautilas, Nudibranches, Jelly fishes, different varieties of Rays, Sharks, Whales and Dolphins comprise the marine wealth of the country.

Point Calimere Wildlife Sanctuary

The Sanctuary is located along the shoreline and hinterland of Indian Ocean, surrounding a saline lagoon in Tamil Nadu. Some Bonnet Macaques, Chitals and Blackbucks are found here. Dolphins and Dugongs are occasionally sighted. The Sanctuary is also famous for the colourful Flamingoes. Some other waders like Oyster-catchers, Black-winged Stilts and Redshanks are found in this region.

GUJARAT

Marine National Park

The Marine National Park is situated along coastal Gujarat in Pirotan Island. It is a virtual paradise for all lovers of marine life. Colourful corals and sponges can be seen underwater. Nudibranches, Barnacles, colourful shells, Sea Anemones, Sea Urchins, Squids, among others, form the colourful

marine life of this National Park. Leather-backed Turtles, Green Sea Turtles and Olive Ridley Turtles come to lay eggs on the sea shore. Hundreds of colourful fishes can be seen in the prisitine waters of this National Park.

Birdlife of this region is spectacular too. The Demoiselle Crane, the Oyster Catcher, the Crab Plover, the Brown and Black-headed Sea Gull are found in large flocks, so are Lesser Flamingoes in the winter months. Other birds found are the Reef and Grey Heron, Black-tailed and Bar-tailed Godwits, the Dunlin and Desert Wheatear.

ORISSA

Chilika

The Sanctuary comprises the lake Chilika, its shore and hinterland. The lagoon of shallow water is separated from the Bay of Bengal by a sandy bar. Scrubby vegetation occurs along the shoreline. A rich mangrove forest is also found here.

The Blackbuck and the Chital can be seen here. Thousands of migratory birds arrive in the lake waters, specially in winter. These include Common Pochards, Gadwalls, Pintails,

Oyster-catchers and Sea Gulls in the Marine National Park, Gujarat.

Page 140: A Green Sea Turtle in the Gulf of Mannar.

Page 141: Nudibranch at Point Calimere.

Shovelers, Pigeons and Tufted Ducks. Pelicans and Flamingoes also arrive during the season. Waders like the Little Stint, the Bar-tailed Godwit, the Dunlin, the Little-ringed Plover and many others can be seen on the shores. Dolphins are often sighted in the mouth of the lagoon.

ANDAMAN AND NICOBAR ISLANDS

Colourful Ankias in Point Calimere Wildlife Sanctuary.

The Andaman and Nicobar Islands comprise a chain of 293 isles scattered across the Pacific Ocean from New Guinea to the Bay of Bengal. The total length of this chain of islands is 725 km. Apart from Car Nicobar, most of the remote islands are hilly with an average altitude of 1,220 m. The isles are covered with dense, verdant tropical forests that have mostly remained virgin and unspoilt. Exceptionally interesting about the Andaman and Nicobars are its aboriginal people and their peculiar customs. The Jarawas are the indigenous people from

these islands and have a population of only 250. The Onges in contrast, are only about 102 in number but are less primitive by nature.

The evergreen forests of the region have endemic animals like the Crab-eating Macaque. The waters of the Andaman and Nicobar support a lot of marine treasures. The colourful sponges and vast coral reefs found here are spectacular. Being an abode of fascinating marine wilderness, the oceanic waters of the Andamans harbour Common and Pacific Dolphins, the Humpback

A bed of colourful Sponges in the Andamans.

LAKSHADWEEP ISLANDS

Whales and Dugongs. Blue Whales, though rare, can be seen here. Among sea turtles, the Olive Ridley Turtles, Green Sea Turtles and Leather-backed Turtles are prominent. Shoals of fishes and Sharks, sea lives like Anemones, colourful Snails, Archens and other organisms have their homes in the marine waters of the Andaman and Nicobar ecosystem. The region boasts of some endemic birds like the Megapode, the Nicobar Pigeon, the Narcondam Hornbill, the Andaman Parakeet, the Andaman Myna and the Andaman Sea Eagle.

In the north of the Indian Ocean lie the emerald islands of Lakshadweep. These islands are parts of the great reefs and volcanic islands of the subcontinent. Among the many small islands, only 10 are inhabited.

Minicoy is the headquarters and the largest of these islands. The lagoons in these islands are relatively shallow. Lakshadweep attracts thousands of foreign tourists every year due to its luxuriant and massive coral reefs. The reefs support innumerable varieties of colourful fishes, Sharks, Dolphins, Dugongs and Whales.

Pacific Dolphins, though rare in the sub-continent, are found in Lakshadweep. It is a paradise for anglers who are interested in Tuna.

Rare birds like the Audubon's Shearwater, the Sooty Tern and the Noddy Tern are found here. The latter two also breed on the Kavaratti Island. The Green Turtle and Leather-backed Turtle nest at Pitti, Minicoy and Suhili Parr Islands.

GULF OF MANNAR

The National Marine Park covers a chain of 21 islands from Rameswaram to Tuticorin. The Centre for Marine Biology has been set up at the island of Kurusadai.

Island in the Gulf of Mannar

This Park was established primarily to conserve corals. The waters of the Gulf harbour Sea Turtles and Dugongs. Beyond Tuticorin, are pearl banks and beds of conches. The priceless Sinistral Shells are found here between June and October.

Top: A shark resting on the sea floor.

Above right: A colourful conch.

Facing page: The Indo-Pacific Dolphin.

BIBLIOGRAPHY

Ali, S, *The Book of Indian Birds*, Bombay Natural History Society, 2002 (revised edition), First edition in 1941

———*The Fall of a Sparrow*, Oxford University Press, 1985 (First edition)

Ali, S and Ripley, D, *The Handbook of Birds of India and Pakistan*, Oxford University Press, 1968-1974

Allen, H, *The Lonely Tiger*, Faber and Faber, London, 1960 (First edition)

Bedi, R, *Indian Wildlife*, Collins Harvill, 1984

Champion, FW, *The Jungle in Sunlight and Shadows*, London, 1925

———*With a Camera in Tiger Land*, London, 1927

Corbett, J, *Man-eaters of Kumaon*, Oxford University Press, 1944

Cubitt, G, Mountfort, G, *Wild India*, London, 1985

Daniel, JC, *The Book of Indian Reptiles*, Bombay Natural History Society, 1983

Fletcher, FWF, *Sports in the Nilgiris and in Wynad*, MacMillan and Co Ltd, London, 1911

Gee, EP, *The Wildlife of India*, Collins, London, 1964

Grimmett, R, Inskipp, C, & T, *Pocket Guide to the Birds of the Indian Subcontinent*, Helm Field Guides, 1999.

Jerdon, TC, *The Birds of India*, Published by Author, Calcutta, 1862-1864

Menon, V, *A Field Guide to Indian Mammals*, Dorling Kindersley, New Delhi, 2003

Prater, SH, *The Book of Indian Animals*, Bombay Natural History Society, 1980 (Third edition)

Roy Chowdhury B, Bhattacharya I, Dasgupta, B, *Wild Wonders of India and Nepal*, Cape Town, 2001

Roy Chowdhury, B, Vyas, P, *A Pictorial Field Guide of the Sunderbans*, New Delhi. 2005

Sankhala, K, *Tigerland*, Collins, London, 1975

Sankhala, K, *Return of the Tiger*, Lustre Press, New Delhi, 1993

Schaller, GB, *The Deer and the Tiger*, The University of Chicago Press, Chicago, 1967

Singh, A, *Tiger Haven*, Oxford University Press, 1973

Thapar, V, *Tiger: Portrait of a Predator*, Facts on File, 1986

Whitaker, R, *Common Indian Snakes*, MacMillan, New Delhi, 1978

Some Important Wildlife and Environmental Societies

Sanctuary Asia
145, 146 Pragati Industrial Estate,
NM Joshi Marg, Lower Parel, Mumbai - 400 011
Tel: +91-22-23016848/49
Sanctuary Asia (Monthly Magazine)

The Bombay Natural History Society (BNHS)
Hornbill House, Dr Salim Ali Chowk,
Shaheed Bhagat Singh Road, Mumbai - 400 001
Tel: +91-22-22821811
BNHS Journal *Hornbill* (Quarterly Magazine)

Centre for Science & Environment (CSE)
41, Tughlakabad Institutional Area, New Delhi - 110 062
Tel: +91-11-29955124/25
Down To Earth (Monthly Magazine)

Chennai Snake Park
Trust Rajbhawan Post, Chennai - 600 002
Tel: +91-44-22353623

Wildlife Institute of India
Post Bag # 18, Chandrabani,
Dehradun - 248 001, Uttarakhand
Tel: +91-135-26401111-15

Wildlife Protection Society of India
S-25, Panchsheel Park, New Delhi - 110 017
Tel: +91-11-41635920/21

Wildlife Trust of India
A-220, New Friends Colony, New Delhi - 110 025
Tel: +91-11-26326025/6

World Wide Fund for Nature—India (WWF)
172 B Lodhi Estate, New Delhi - 110 003
Tel: +91-11-41504786

Ranthambhore Foundation
19, Kautilya Marg
Chanakyapuri, New Delhi - 110 021
Tel: +91-11-23016261

Wildlife Preservation Society of India
7 Astley Hall,
Dehradun - 248 001, Uttarakhand
Tel: +91-135-226508

Rhino Foundation
Girish Bordolai Path, Bamunimaidam,
Guwahati - 781 021, Assam

Assam Valley Wildlife Society
Pertabghur Tea Estate, PO Chariali, Assam
Tel: +91-3715-2074

Nature Environment & Wildlife Society
10, Chowringhee Terrace, Kolkata - 700 020
Tel: +91-33-22234148
Environ (Quarterly Magazine)

Prakriti Samsad
65 Golf Club Road, Kolkata - 700 033
Tel: +91-33-24235058
The Naturalist (Annual Publication)

Photo Credits

Acknowledgements

My grateful thanks to Pradeep Vyas who unhesitatingly extended his co-operation and to all photographers who have contributed their photographs in this book.

My gratitude to Ajanta Dey and Partha Dey, and to Chitra Shome and Barnali Roy, for the enormous effort they put in towards the making of this book.

Koustubh Sharma, a wildlife expert in his own right, was very generous with his valuable inputs, and Supriya Mukherjee cared for this book as though it were her own. My gratitude to both for their committment to the cause of wildlife.

Last but not least, I thank Bikash D Niyogi, Utpal Shome and Virendra Kumar for translating a dream into reality.

INDEX